How to Greatly
Influence your Child
While Parenting

HOW TO GREATLY
INFLUENCE YOUR CHILD
WHILE PARENTING

A.S. BAMANIA

authorHOUSE®

AuthorHouse™ UK Ltd.
1663 Liberty Drive
Bloomington, IN 47403 USA
www.authorhouse.co.uk
Phone: 0800.197.4150

Published by AuthorHouse 01/09/2014

ISBN: 978-1-4918-9051-6 (sc)
ISBN: 978-1-4918-9050-9 (hc)
ISBN: 978-1-4918-9052-3 (e)

CONTENTS

Introduction.. v

    How This Book Was Written and Why v

    What Is This Book About? vi

Chapter 1: Expectations... 1

    Establishing Expectations for Your Child..................... 1

    Expectations Which Should Be Avoided..................... 2

    Exactly What Can Be Done? 3

    How to Help Your Child Meet Your Expectations.......... 5

    Effort Expectations 6

    What to Do When Your Expectations Aren't Met.......... 7

    Exactly How Can We Offer This Needed
Supplement?... 9

Chapter 2: The Stages from Birth to Adolescence..................... 11

    Infancy 11

    Toddler... 13

    Pre-School... 15

    Preparatory School 17

    Adolescence... 19

Chapter 3: Communication 24

    Communicating with Young Children 24

    Babies and Toddlers: Ages up to Two 24

    Pre-Schoolers: Ages Two to Five.............................. 27

    School-Age Children: Ages Six to Eleven 30

    Teen Years from Twelve to Eighteen......................... 33

Chapter 4: Behaviour.. 42

    Three Types of Behaviour... 42

    Why Children Misbehave 44

    What Can I Do to Change My Child's Behaviour?...... 45

Chapter 5: Rules... 51

    Establishing House Rules for Teenagers..................... 51

    Rules that Promote Safety 51

Rules That Teach Morality 52
Rules That Encourage Healthy Habits......................... 53
Rules That Prepare Teenagers for the Real World........ 53
Rules That Enhance Social Skills 54

Chapter 6: Child Safety First 55
Child Safety First: The First Year.............................. 55
Child Safety First: Ages One and Two...................... 56
Child Safety First: Ages Two and Three 57
Child Safety First: Ages Three to Five...................... 57
Child Safety First: Ages Six to Eight 58
Child Safety First: Ages Nine to Eleven.................... 59
Child Safety First: Ages Twelve to Fourteen 59
Child Safety First: Ages Fifteen to Seventeen 60
Top Internet Safety Tips for Parents 61

Chapter 7: Overcoming Laziness in Children.................. 65

Chapter 8: Habits 70
Advice on Compulsive Habits.................................. 70
Why Do Habits Form? 71
Bad Habits/Annoying Behaviour 71
Bad Habits and Behaviours in Children 71
How to Break Your Child's Bad Habit........................ 77
How to Cope.. 78
Every Child Is Different.. 79

Chapter 9: Teaching Kids about Money 80
Allow Them to Earn Money 80
Develop a Budgeting Plan 81
Setting Goals 82
Provide Consequences When Necessary 82
Useful Tips on Teaching Kids about Money 82

Chapter 10: Reward Systems 85
Reward Systems for Toddlers and Pre-Schoolers........ 85
Reward Systems for School-Age Children 85
Reward Systems for Tweens 86
Reward Systems for Teenagers 87

Chapter 11: Punishment and Discipline......................... 88
What Is Punishment? 88

The Problems with Punishments 89
What Is Discipline?..89
The Biggest Discipline Mistakes Parents Make 90
Parenting Mistakes...93
Types of Parenting Styles..94
Determining a Discipline Strategy 96
Positive Discipline Techniques.................................96
Self-Discipline 99

Chapter 12: Helping Children Deal with Their Anger.............103
Controlling Anger and Resentment 103
Helping Kids Learn Self-Control...............................106
Tips on Teaching Your Teen How to
Deal with Stress...107

Chapter 13: Social Skills..109
How to Develop Social Skills in Children 109
Useful Ways to Boost Your Child's Social Skills 112

Chapter 14: Confidence...116
Kids and Self-Esteem..116
What Is Self-Esteem?..118
How to Help Your Child Have Self-Esteem and
Be Self-Confident...120
Things to Remember...127

Key Points...129

INTRODUCTION

How This Book Was Written and Why

In order to explain precisely how and why this book was written, I have to go back to my past. When I was young, I had to take care of my cousin's two daughters and son. They were still babies between one and three years old. I spent lot of time with my cousin's children after coming home from work; I was kind of babysitting them. I observed that my cousin used to get frustrated with her kids and used to raise her voice and say, "No, do not touch that!" or "You are always naughty!"

During that time I saw on TV a show about raising the baby. It made a superb statement which touched my heart and soul. The presenter said, "If you stop your kids doing anything when they are still in their childhood, their curiosity will stop. It will not let them develop their mind." This statement opened my eyes. I immediately ran to my cousin and made her watch that program. Immediately I saw a different person in my cousin. Her way of looking at her kids changed. She became more concerned about her kids than before. She bought some books that increased my interest as well. We used to read them and share ideas.

Later I moved from my cousin's house and went to live at a friend's place for some time. Wherever I went—in a supermarket or shopping centre or on the bus or on the road—I would see parents shouting at their kids and not treating them the way they should be treated to make them better people. I have seen parents quarrelling and swearing in front of their kid. Just imagine the future of that child. This gave me the idea to share what I have learned from books, TV shows, and other resources.

After I left my cousin's house, a colleague from my workplace needed someone for babysitting. I said, "I would like to help you. I miss my cousin's kids, and I love kids."

The next day I met my colleague's kids. I decided to make these children better people. However, time passed by and there was not much improvement, so I started to ask myself what was going wrong. It was not long before a thought came to me. I said to myself, "It's the parents." They spent most of their time with their kids, and they were the first heroes of their children. They were teaching the difference between wrong and right. They were the ones who could make a big difference in their kids' lives.

So I began to write and to share my ideas. First I shared with my family, friends, and colleagues from work. To my surprise, they said it was helpful and was making them more knowledgeable. They changed the way they looked at and talked with their kids, and they reported that their children were changing as well.

One day I was sitting at a restaurant having a great lunch, when I heard a mother and daughter screaming at each other because the mom had caught the daughter smoking a cigarette. Nearby people were looking at them.

I believed a change could be made without shouting at the daughter. Just a small talk with some planning can change a kid into a better person. So I decided to share my ideas with parents all over the world.

What Is This Book About?

This book is awesome! For those of you who are serious about having more, doing more, and being more, this book can help you tremendously. If you are looking to change your results and do so quickly, then read this book. Buy copies for those you love. They will thank you for a long time.

Raising a baby, specifically for the first time, is both interesting and tough. This is a time for developing bonds that will last a lifetime, a time to offer the child the internal sources necessary to build self-esteem and the capability to connect positively with others. It is likewise the moment for parents to start to discover who this new individual really is. Each child is unique. It is vital that moms and dads discover, respect, support, and encourage the distinct qualities and potentials of each youngster.

My main goal in writing this book is to help parents to understand what their children need and what they want, and to know what to expect as children grow from babies to adolescents. It will help you as a parent understand why they behave in different ways and what you can do to change it. The main purpose of this book is to develop a great person out of your child.

This book will assist you in solving problems with your child. You will be making the right decisions for your child in creating ways and means of great achievement. With the techniques in this book, you can sleep on it and awake in the morning with answers so clear-cut you will be amazed!

As human beings, we sometimes forget things. It will be a good idea if your make your own notes or highlight the main points from this book. I also encourage you to read this book over and over as it will make you understand better.

Prepare yourself for a wonderful experience. Just look around and you'll see how few parents really know what they want from their child or how they're guiding their own child. Having no goal in mind for their kids, they can't even discern the difference between what is good for them and what is bad.

If you too are that way—don't worry! This book is going to change you and help your child to be a better person.

Chapter 1:

EXPECTATIONS

Establishing Expectations for Your Child

Parental expectations can have a strong effect on kids' motivations and assumptions about themselves. While realistic and healthy expectations can urge children to success, unrealistically high expectations can set children up for failure. Such unrealistic expectations can also bring about anxiety and discouragement when a kid can not measure up to her mom's and dads' objectives. Similarly, low expectations can make it difficult for children to determine and achieve their full capacity.

Teenagers will likely act miserable when their moms and dads put expectations on them. Nonetheless, they generally need to understand that their parents care sufficiently about them to anticipate certain standards, such as good grades, appropriate habits, and adherence to the regulations of the house. Adolescents will likely try to meet these standards if moms and dads have proper expectations. Without sensible expectations, your teen may feel you don't care about him or her.

Establishing expectations for your kids is an important duty of parenting. Expectations inform children exactly what's important to you and set up a specification goal toward which your children can aim. But assumptions can also be double-edged swords. They can be an incredible advantage to your children's development, but they can also cause crushing problems that hamper growth. It depends on what types of assumptions you establish for them. Sadly, the society of success that permeates popular culture has actually persuaded lots of parents to establish the wrong kind of assumptions for their youngsters.

1

Parental expectations can have a solid effect on kids' inspirations and self-expectations. While healthy and sensible expectations can motivate excellence in little ones, unrealistically high assumptions can set kids up for failure.

Expectations Which Should Be Avoided

Improbable adult assumptions usually originate from parents' own childhoods. A lot of moms and dads frequently try to make up for the unmet needs of their own youth by establishing assumptions for their kids based upon their own encounters rather than on their kids' requirements. Moms and dads who were dissatisfied with their own academic performance may stress high scholastic accomplishment in their kids. Generally, parents need to be mindful of their children's distinct necessities and strengths, as well as to exercise self-awareness when establishing expectations.

There are two types of expectations that you should not set for your kids: ability and result expectations. Ability expectations are those where youngsters are anticipated to achieve a specific outcome as a result of their innate ability. "We expect you to obtain straight As since you're so wise" or "We expect you to succeed due to the fact that you're the best sportsmen out there." The problem with ability assumptions is that youngsters have no command over their capability. Children are born with a particular amount of ability, and all they can do is take full advantage of whatever capacity they are given. The truth is that if your children aren't satisfying your ability assumptions, you have no one to criticize but yourself. You didn't provide them sufficient genes. An additional trouble with potential assumptions is that if kids connect their excellences to their capacity—"I gained due to the fact that I'm so gifted"—they have to attribute their failings to their absence of capacity—"I failed because I'm dumb." And you cannot alter foolishness!

Popular society stresses outcomes over all else. Therefore, moms and dads often establish result expectations where their kids are anticipated to generate a certain result. "We expect you to succeed in this game" or "We know you'll be the first-chair violin in the orchestra." The issue is that, once again, youngsters are asked to fulfil an expectation over which they may not have control. They might execute to the best of their capacity, but they still may not fulfil your result expectations due to the fact that another child did much better. So they would need to consider themselves as having actually fallen short, even though they gave a great performance. Setting outcome assumptions also conveys to your children that you value outcomes over everything else, so they'll involve judge themselves by the exact same requirements. Unlike what you may think, capability and result expectations really hinder your kid's success efforts.

Exactly What Can Be Done?

Now you may be thinking, "Wait a minute! I cannot push my little ones to obtain excellent grades or do their best at school, in sporting activities, and in various other pursuits? No chance I'm buying this." Before you jump all over me, allow me to clear and deliver all these concepts.

Today we all have to recognize a basic reality: results matter! There are no two ways about it. In most of our society, people are actually judged on the results they create—grades, revenues, success, and profits. Though it would certainly be wonderful if we all made money based on our good intentions and efforts, that is not the way the world functions. However, this societal emphasis may induce you moms and dads to set your wants when it comes to your kids' success. After all, we all want to do the best when it comes to our youngsters.

I would certainly recommend that you quit result requirements completely, but still provide your kids something I refer to as "outcome goals". Objectives are quite various through assumptions. Result assumptions are typically set by parents and placed in front of their little ones without their input, and kids normally feel they are being dragged, sometimes kicking and screaming, toward those assumptions. Kids have no ownership of the assumption and little inspiration, other than a recommended threat from their moms and dads, to satisfy the expectations.

When I talk to little ones about assumptions, they generally grimace and claim things like "That's when my mom and dad get really involved, I learn they are actually going to tax me" or perhaps "They are actually telling me what to perform, and I'd better do this or I'll get in trouble." Not precisely "feel-good" parenting! End-result requirements are actually black or white; your children either comply with the assumption and they thrive, or they do not and they fail. There is actually incredibly little opportunity when it comes to excellence and lots of space for failure.

Objectives are completely different. I think that youngsters are wired to react to targets. Among the greatest happiness in life is to set a target, pursue a goal, and achieve an objective. Children tend to set objectives for themselves, with advice from parents, coaches, and teachers. And they intend to go after those goals. Targets aren't black and white; they offer degrees of attainment. Not every objective is accomplished, yet there will certainly be constant improvement towards an objective for which progress determines excellence. So if youngsters provide their best effort, there is little possibility of failure and an excellent opportunity for excellence. When I ask little ones about objectives, they react quite differently. Their faces perk up, and they say things like "It indicates I am determined to do something, and I really work doggedly to do it" or "I really feel like my parents are behind me and I'm very keen to do it."

For instance, a kid's mom and dad developed an outcome expectation of raising her math grade from 75 to 90 during the school year. She would certainly have fallen short of complying with the result expectation if she just boosted her grade to 88, but if she set an outcome target, then though the goal of a 90 had not been totally achieved, she would still determine the 88 a success—as well she should.

Lots of parents believe that results at a youthful age are necessary, so they stress outcomes and place outcome expectations on their youngsters. Yet childhood is all about finding out, improving, creating, and getting the abilities, perspectives, and worth needed for later success. Using objectives instead of assumptions is one of the best ways to cultivate this growth.

But even outcome targets aren't perfect. Lots of parents believe that concentrating on the result will raise the chances of that result occurring, but the opposite is in fact true. Here's why. When does the result of an effort appear (e.g., in a test or a sports competition)? At the end of a program. And if kids are focusing on completion of the performance, what are they not concentrating on? Well, the procedure, undoubtedly. Here's the irony. By concentrating on the procedure rather than the outcome, your kids will most likely perform securely and, if they continue securely, they're most likely to accomplish the result you wanted in the first place. Also, why are children stressed prior to a test, sporting event, or recital? Because they worry about the result, or more particularly, because they fear failure. By getting them to concentrate on the result, they're less likely to perform well and achieve the outcome you wanted for them.

If you're going to establish results, set outcome goals, but then immediately direct your youngster's emphasis into the process, that is, exactly what they need to do to accomplish the desired outcome.

How to Help Your Child Meet Your Expectations

Adult assumptions are a key to discipline in little ones. When combined with loving, supportive attitudes, establishing clear behaviour and scholastic expectations for kids can assist them discover manners, social capabilities, research abilities, and various other tools they will need to prosper in university and life. However, for expectations to bring about good habits, adult policies and ideas regarding correct behaviour need to be age-appropriate and take account of the youngster's maturity level and skills. If regulations and expectations go far beyond a kid's capabilities, they may lead to stress and anxiety or insubordinate habits. Hence, moms and dads need to think about each kid's unique capabilities and constraints when setting up expectations.

Effort Expectations

If you desire your kids to be successful, instead of setting result expectations, you need to establish effort assumptions, over which they have control and which actually urge them to do what it takes to attain the results you desire. These assumptions are within your kids' control. They are a lot a lot more likely to embrace and pursue them if your youngsters feel that they have the tools to attain their objectives. Consider exactly what your children have to do to become successful, and develop effort assumptions that will lead to their excellence: commitment, effort, discipline, patience, concentration, determination, and good attitudes. "Our family expects you to offer your best initiative" or "Our family expects you to make your studies a top priority." These assumptions are beneficial, whether someone is making the effort to be an expert, educator, professional sportsman, writer, parent, spouse, or artist. Beyond the capacities they inherited from you, youngsters have the ability to make use of initiative assumptions and the devices connected with them to be the best they can be in whatever position they choose to pursue.

Effort assumptions should be developed in partnership with your children. This participation technique ensures that your children have ownership of the assumptions, as opposed to feeling that you have simply placed the assumptions on them. You can discuss with your youngsters about the value of effort, exactly how it will certainly help them to achieve their goals. You can tell them that they are in the catbird seat when it comes to their effort. You could share examples with your children of how remarkable people used the power of effort to become effective. Most important, you should help them make the connection between their efforts and success.

If your children fulfil your effort expectations, they will, in all likelihood, execute well, accomplish some degree of success, and gain satisfaction in their initiatives. Exactly how effective they become will depend on what capabilities they were born with. They will certainly benefit from your approval, excellent grades, and enhanced performance in various other activities. If your youngsters don't fulfil the initiative expectations, they might not do well and need to experience the repercussions, including your disapproval, inadequate grades, and so on. They will certainly be disappointed—they need to be! However, rather than being crushed by the failure, they will understand that they have the power to fulfil the assumptions in the future. Meeting their effort expectations will certainly motivate your kids to set higher effort expectations.

What to Do When Your Expectations Aren't Met

When you were pregnant, what did you imagine your kid would be like? Were you thinking boy or girl? Would he look like his father? Would she have your blonde hair? She is kicking a great deal, so does this mean she'll be a sportsman? An essential component of maternity is the connection you make with your thought of the baby.

When the long-awaited day comes and the real child shows up, the envisioned child doesn't disappear altogether. An early challenge of new parenthood is taking care of the disparity between the visualized and the actual child. And this is an obstacle that will certainly be revisited at various stages of a kid's development. At times, without realizing it, we compare the kid we have with the child we envisioned we would have, and the pictured youngster is keeping us from understanding our actual child.

One fact is obvious: you have a son or a daughter. But such an obvious truth could be a stumbling block if a mother constantly visualized having a child of a specific gender. One mother of a girl, who had really desired a boy, ended up being committed to non-sexist child rearing. She purchased her little girl toy vehicles and dressed her in pants. Needless to say, her daughter fell for dresses and declined to wear pants, leading to an on-going disagreement with her mother.

Parents often claim they want their children to be who they are rather than fulfil some adult desire about who or what they should be. But without understanding it, this objective is sometimes thwarted by issues left over from mom or dad's own life.

One mother who, as a young person, had pushed away good friends by being too controlling, was determined to avoid repeating this mistake with her daughter. She stifled several of her daughter's habits which, although not bad habits, seemed "bossy" to her because of her fear that they might cause the same result she had experienced as a kid.

A father recognized his boy's good attributes with his own readiness to accept how others addressed him, no matter just how poorly. He looked for ways to help his boy become a lot more assertive, driving him into karate and criticizing cooperative behaviour that he thought of as conciliatory.

Due to the fact that they remember difficult relationships with their own siblings, moms and dads sometimes worry about sibling rivalry. Their resolve to develop good partnerships amongst their children prompts such strong responses to the most common rivalry that the children come to be more resentful of each other.

Sometimes we try to renovate our own lives, mend our mistakes, or accomplish passions we had given up via our youngsters. Maybe we imagine that the very road we did not take will be followed by our youngster. Failing to excel at a certain topic in school or to develop a longed-for skill is seen by moms and dads, and consequently by the kids, as a weakness.

Both bad expectations (the expectancy of attributes we don't wish to accept) and favourable expectations (the passions we long for in our kids) can be similarly intrusive in the advancement of the actual child. Behaviour seen from the perspective of a negative assumption is usually deemed troubled behaviour. Despite out best intentions, we may try to repair something in our child merely because we identify it with something we don't like in ourselves. We have difficulty seeing our child as a person separate from ourselves.

Similarly, if we are focused on having a kid accomplish some passion of our own—to stand out in sports or achieve adequate grades for a particular college, for example—we can fail to support a youngster in developing his or her own unique capacities or positive characteristics. Acknowledging and giving approval to kids for their abilities and toughness is the needed supplement for advancement.

Exactly How Can We Offer This Needed Supplement?

Don't fool yourself into thinking that you have obvious wishes for your child. Facing them directly will help you separate them from who your youngster really is.

Think about your own life and recognize that your youngster is entitled to have her own. You are not your mom and your kid is not you. Her life will be different from yours.

Recognize exactly what your child excels at and concentrate on that, even if you don't agree with it at all.

All children get stuck at specific points. This is not the perfect youngster you envisioned. Moms and dads are also educators, and the very best way to educate is to start where a child is. Do not get caught up in your own frustration, but rather consider how to help your youngster move ahead.

- It is neither their failure nor yours when kids need assistance.

- Appreciate your child for who he is, not for who you pictured he would be!
- Be clear in describing expectations.

At this point please read this chapter again to understand more clearly and then proceed to the next one. Remember to make some notes about what you think is interesting and important.

Chapter 2:

THE STAGES FROM BIRTH TO ADOLESCENCE

Throughout the first year of your child's life, she will go from an ignorant new born who has little motor control to an infant on the verge of toddling. This first phase of child development includes fast physical development that supports her brand new capabilities. Major turning points consist of rolling over at approximately four to six months, sitting up unassisted by six months old, and crawling and even walking by one year. By the end of the baby stage, children have great motor abilities to use a pincer grasp, get and take down small objects, and try to scribble with a crayon or other writing device. You will also observe, as your child reaches four to six months, that she will start to actively babble and laugh or squeal with emotion. By twelve months, an infant may also have the capacity to say basic words, such as "mama" and comprehend a limited lexicon of basic words such as "no".

Infancy

The first development stage is from one to three months. During this stage, infants' bodies and brains are discovering external factors. Between birth and three months, your child could start to:

- Smile. At first it will be simply to herself. However, within three months she will be smiling in response to your smiles and attempting to get you to smile back at her.
- When on her tummy, raise her head and chest.
- Track items with her eyes and slowly reduce eye crossing.
- Open and shut her hands and bring her hands to her mouth.
- Grip objects in her hands.

- Take swipes at or reach for hanging items, though she generally won't be able to get them.

Between four and six months, babies are really discovering how to reach out and control the world around them. They're mastering the use of those amazing devices, their hands. And they're finding their voices. From four to six months old, your baby will most likely:

- Roll over from front to back or back to front. Front-to-back typically comes first.
- Babble, making noises that can sound like genuine language.
- Laugh.
- Connect to and grab for items. (Watch out for your hair!) Manipulate toys and various other objects with her hands.
- Sit up with support and have terrific head control.

During the second half of the first year, your kid becomes a child on the go. After discovering that he can get somewhere by rolling over, he'll spend the next few months determining the best ways to relocate forward or backwards. Better get on it if you haven't baby-proofed yet!

Between seven and nine months, your infant will:

- Begin to crawl. This can include scooting (moving around on his bottom) or "arm crawling" (dragging himself on his tummy by arms and legs), as well as conventional crawling on hands and knees. Some children never ever crawl, moving straight to from scooting to walking.
- Sit without support.
- React to familiar words like his name. He might likewise reply to "no" by briefly stopping and looking at you, and could begin babbling "mama" and "dada".
- Clap and play games such as patty-cake and peekaboo.
- Discover how to move to a standing position.

The last development phase in a child's first year, from ten to twelve months, is quite a change. She isn't a baby any longer, and she may look and act more like a young child. However she's still an infant in many ways. She's discovering how to:

- Begin feeding herself. Babies at this stage of development master the "pincer grasp"; they can hold small items such as O-shaped cereal between their thumb and forefinger.
- Cruise, or walk around the space on her feet while holding on to the furniture.
- Say one or two words, and "mama" and "dada" become definite names for mom and dad. The average is about three spoken words by the first birthday, but this varies enormously.
- Point at objects she wants in order to get your attention.
- Start "make-believe play" by copying you or using objects correctly, such as pretending to chat on the phone.
- Take her first steps. This usually takes place right around one year, but it can vary significantly.

During this time, your kid is becoming considerably much more mobile and knowledgeable about herself and her surroundings. Her desire to check out new items and individuals is likewise improving. During this phase, your kid will certainly show greater self-reliance, begin to reveal bold habits, acknowledge herself in pictures or a mirror, and replicate the behaviour of others, particularly grownups and older youngsters.

Your toddler will likewise have the ability to acknowledge labels of familiar individuals and items, kind easy expressions and sentences, and follow basic directions and instructions.

Toddler

Because your child's growing need is to state his independence, this stage is commonly called the "terrible twos". This can be a stimulating time for you and your young child. He will experience big intellectual, social, and psychological adjustments that will certainly help him explore his brand new world and understand it.

At this stage, your toddler will have the ability to follow two- or three-phrase commands, sort things by form and colour, replicate the actions of grownups and friends, and show a large range of feelings.

Between one and three years of ages, your kid is making major strides towards self-reliance. Youngsters are up on their feet strolling and running. By twenty-four months, many kids can kick a ball, go up and down stairs with assistance, and hold things while moving. Young children can also scribble, making marks that they see as actual things, develop block towers, and start to feed themselves. Language and interaction skills develop sharply at this stage; commonly a two-year-old understands between five and seven hundred words and speaks more than five hundred words. Socially and emotionally, kids are immature, having less self-control when "playing" with peers. For instance, it's not unusual for a toddler to strike or scream when sharing a toy with another youngster.

During this phase, your kid will certainly show greater freedom, start to reveal bold habits, acknowledge himself in images or a mirror, and copy the habits of others, especially grownups and older kids.

At eighteen months, most children will:

- Walk well with feet somewhat apart.
- Climb up, managing edges and challenges well.
- Claim six to twelve recognizable words.
- Copy valid points of sentences.
- Desire to be a lot more independent and do things without support.
- Show personality type.
- Play alone, but still seek to be near grownups.
- Get angry and throw tantrums.
- Make use of things and routines for comfort and safety.

At two years children can:

- Walk up staircases and possibly walk backwards.
- Bow and stand without using hands.
- Throw and kick a ball over arm.
- Claiming fifty or even more recognizable words and comprehend a lot more.
- Can sing some tunes.
- Be increasingly independent yet still continuously demand their mom's and dad's attention.
- Cling snugly in devotion, burn out, or fear.
- When irritated, throw temper tantrums.
- Beginning to create a creative imagination.

By the age of three years most children:

- Identify some images by naming them.
- Stand on one foot, walk on tiptoes, and walk upstairs.
- Constantly ask questions.
- Pay attention to and tell stories.
- Wash and dry their hands.
- Identify a friend by name.
- Use much less "baby talk" in speech.
- Speak in an understandable way half the time.
- Have fewer temper tantrums.
- Develop anxieties about the dark or pets.

Get in touch with your maternal and child health registered nurse about emotional development in your young child whether they are caring and if they relate to you for convenience or if you have concerns about language advancement, the variety of words your toddler knows and speaks, and also how he tries to put words together.

Pre-School

Even if your youngster doesn't go to an official pre-school program, the ages between three and five are generally called the pre-school years. By the age of four, a lot of kids move well, stand and jump on one foot, kick a softball effortlessly, and even toss a ball overhand. By five, youngsters might even get on play devices, somersault, and dodge. In addition, the pre-schooler's growing motor and cognitive abilities permit her to draw geometric shapes, patterns, and human beings and create some letters of the alphabet. Emotionally, the pre-schooler is developing better self-regulation capacities and has the capability to verbally share exactly what she is really feeling, as opposed to just making use of motions or physical aggression. Socially, pre-schoolers are entering a brand new world where they are making their very first real friends based on similar interests. They have the ability to share and take turns and can reveal empathy toward others.

Between the ages of three and four, children can:

- Hang out with a more comprehensive array of people.
- Know how to share and play well with other children.
- Develop a sense of humour and a concern for others.
- Use fingers and hands skilfully.
- Hold a pencil in a fully grown hold using preferred hand.
- Speak well.
- Throw fewer tantrums.

Between four to five years, they:

- Ask intricate questions.
- Improve their walking, running, and climbing skills.
- Learn to use a bicycle with training wheels.
- Enhance their drawing skills and learn to write some numbers and letters.
- Understand the meaning of numbers.
- Develop relationships with peers.
- Show self-reliance but may become irritated when exhausted, ashamed, or angry.
- Reveal self-confidence and greater skill and speed in physical capabilities.
- Have prolonged discussions.

Preparatory School

From about the age of six through the early teenage years, children are generally thought of as grade-school children. At this stage, as the name says, children enter preparatory school. Throughout the early years of grammar school, children might rely more on their parents for their social and emotional necessities. However, as the child moves toward the teenage years, peers begin to play larger functions in his or her life. Physically, grade school children have the gross motor capacities to deal with brand new types of movement, such as sporting activities or dancing lessons, as well as fine motor skills that enable them to draw and write the alphabet. Grade school youngsters also begin to take on more scholastic duties and know the rudiments of education that they will use throughout their life, such as mathematics, language, composing, and science.

Six and seven year olds:

- Take pleasure in a lot of tasks and stay busy.
- Like to draw and paint.
- Might lose their first tooth.
- Have vision as sharp as an adult's vision.
- Develop skills in order to come to be better.
- Jump rope and ride a bike.
- Know the concept of numbers.
- Understand night time and day time.
- Know their right and left hands.
- Can copy complicated shapes, such as a diamond.
- Can tell time.
- Can understand commands with three separate instructions.
- Can describe objects and their usage.
- Can repeat three numbers backwards.
- Can review age-appropriate publications and/or products.
- Share and cooperate, but will cheat if able.
- Are jealous of siblings and others.
- Like to copy grownups.

- Like to play alone, but good friends are becoming important.
- Play with good friends of the same gender.
- May have tantrums.
- Have moderate concern for their physical body.
- Like to play parlour games.

Eight to nine year olds:

- Are more graceful in their movements and potentials.
- Leap, skip, and chase.
- Grooms and dresses themselves completely.
- Can make use of devices, e.g., hammer, screwdriver.
- Can count in reverse.
- Understand the date.
- Read even more and enjoy reading.
- Comprehend portions.
- Know the idea of room.
- Attract and paint.
- Can say the months and days of week in order.
- Take pleasure in collecting items.
- Like competitions and games.
- Begin to play and make friends with kids of the opposite gender.
- Are modest concerning the physical body.
- Enjoy teams and clubs, such as Boy Scouts or Lady Scouts.
- Becoming curious about boy-girl connections, but do not admit it.

Between ten and twelve years old, children:

- Grow the rest of their adult teeth.
- Like to sew and paint.
- Make up stories.
- Like to write letters.
- Review well.
- Delight in using the telephone.
- See good friends as vital; could have a best friend.

- Show increased interest in the opposite sex.
- Like and value their moms and dads.
- Delight in getting in touch with others.

Adolescence

In this section, I will describe the development that twelve- to fifteen-years-olds go through.

In physical terms, children of this age experience the following.

- They continue to grow taller and bigger.
- Girls start breast development between the ages of nine and thirteen.
- Girls begin menstruation at an average age of twelve and three quarters.
- Boys' testes start to increase in size of between the ages of nine and a half and thirteen and a half.
- Skin adjustments may take place. These can cause breakouts of acne and can be uncomfortable.

These changes can be difficult for children. They may start to feel awkward concerning their bodies. Talk with your child concerning modifications that will happen, and pay attention to your child's feelings about these adjustments.

Adolescents also go through a lot of emotional development. Mood swings may be typical throughout this period; you kid may go from happy to mad in one minute!

Preteens and young teens may really feel emotions a lot more intensely compared to adults. Your child is most likely to be more impulsive than an adult would be.

Preteens and youthful teens might be uncomfortable with these new feelings—just as awkward as you are).

Cognitively, adolescents experience an increase in abstract thinking. Your kid will have the ability to anticipate what will happen as opposed to what just did happen. Your child can now think and speculate, and your youngster is now more likely to doubt your values and regulations rather than to follow them simply because "you said so".

Things may frequently appear unjust to your kid.

In terms of social development, friends become crucial. These friends can be both unfavourable and favourable influences.

Involvement in secret clubs or teams is common, Your child may keep secrets from you; this is normal and must not be bothersome unless you see signs of unsafe behaviours. The adolescent invests much less time with his or her household and might be embarrassed to be around moms and dads. This is normal and a form of freedom. Allow your child to understand that you still wish to hang around together *and* that you want them to learn to be independent.

Because of physical changes and concerns about fitting in with good friends, your kid may lose self-esteem or confidence during this time.

There are several things to watch out for in terms of the health of the adolescent. You may see the following:

- Signs of depression.
- Relentless sensations of stress and anxiety, emptiness, or despair
- Sensations of hopelessness and/or gloom.
- Feelings of guilt, pointlessness, or helplessness.
- Antsy behaviour or short temper.
- Dislike of activities and hobbies that used to be pleasurable.
- Reduction in energy, feeling of fatigue.
- Problems focusing, deciding, and remembering specifics.

- Modifications in sleep patterns or insomnia, waking up too early, or sleeping way too much.
- Changes in appetite patterns, loss of appetite, or over-eating.
- Thoughts of self-destruction, attempts at suicide.
- Aches, pains, stomach troubles that are relentless and are not eliminated with treatment.

The adolescent years bring a lot of changes, not only physically but also psychologically and socially. Throughout these years, teens boost their ability to think abstractly and ultimately make strategies and set lasting goals. Each kid might progress at a different rate and may have a different view of the world. In general, the following are some of the possibilities that might be evident in your adolescent:

- Establishes the ability to think abstractly.
- Is concerned with philosophy, national politics, and social concerns.
- Forms lasting beliefs.
- Establishes objectives.
- Contrasts his or herself with peers.

As your adolescent begins to have difficulty in terms of self-reliance and control, a lot of changes may occur. The following are some of the concerns that may arise with your teen during these years:

- Wants independence from mom and dad.
- Peer impact and approval becomes very important.
- Male-female relationships become vital.
- Could be in love.
- Has long-lasting commitment in relationship.

Here is a list of what to expect between the ages of eleven and nineteen.

- Adolescents use much longer sentences, generally ten to fifteen words or more.
- They know how to use sarcasm, and they know when others are being sarcastic to them.
- They are able to change topics in conversations.
- They use more subtle and witty humour.
- They have some understanding of idioms, such as "put your money where your mouth is!"
- They know that they talk differently to good friends than to teachers.
- They understand and use slang terms with their buddies. They keep up with quickly changing "street talk".
- They can follow complicated guidelines.
- When they have not understood something, they will ask to be told again.
- They can easily switch in between "class" talk and "break-time" talk.
- They tell long and extremely challenging stories.
- They have basically finished physical growth; their physical components are now basically designed and defined.
- It is more likely that they will act on their sexual desires.
- They feel stress over failure.
- They may appear moody, angry, lonely, spontaneous, self-centred, confused, and/or persistent.
- They experience contrasting feelings of dependence and independence.
- Their relationships range from pleasant to unfavourable with mom and dad.
- They occasionally really feel that moms and dads are "as well interested".
- Normally, they have many pals and few confidantes, though this differs significantly based on their degree of maturity. They could be awkward or enjoy activities with the opposite sex.
- They might enjoy a single, charming relationship.
- They may lack information concerning or self-assurance relating to their personal abilities and capacities.

- They become seriously concerned about the future; they start to incorporate understanding and make choices about their future.
- They are disappointed and confused about the inconsistencies between the claimed benefits and the actual behaviours of their family and/or good friends; they experience sensations of stress, isolation, sorrow, and anger.
- They could be interested in sex in response to physical and emotional stimuli and as a method to participate in the grownup world (but not necessarily as an expression of fully grown intimacy).

The teen years mark a significant separation in advancement, as the youngster starts to look and act more like an adult than a child. At the beginning of the teenage years, kids will certainly go through a set of physical modifications called adolescence. This includes the onset of menstruation, the growth of body hair and in boys a voice modification. Teenagers normally aim to become much more independent and frequently focus much more on friendships and romantic partnerships than relationships with their immediate family. Additionally, teenagers may look towards their adult future and check out a potential occupation with teaching fellowships or after-school tasks.

- Always remember that no child develops in the same way or at the same speed as another child.
- This time period may be more challenging for your child if he or she has always reacted badly to change in his or her life.
- Remember to be involved with your child. Your opinion and support still matter

Now you have a better understanding of your child's expectations and the behaviour of your child. Read this chapter again; it will help you better to understand the rest of the book.

Chapter 3:

COMMUNICATION

Communicating with Young Children

Communicating well with children helps them establish confidence, self-regard, and good connections with others. It likewise helps make life with young children much more enjoyable for moms and dads as wells as youngsters.

Positive interaction concentrates on respect for the kid and involves both speaking and listening. Interaction is simply what we say and how we say it. Good interaction results in nurturing connections, cooperation, and feelings of worth. Poor interaction can cause little ones who "turn off" adults and have problems and squabbles and feelings of worthlessness.

When feelings are involved—either their own or the child's—adults often have trouble interacting positively with youngsters. There are ways for parents to improve their interaction with children.

Get the child's attention before speaking. Children can only focus on one thing at a time. Look straight at the child and call her name. Touching on the shoulder or taking her hand will certainly help get her attention. Allow her time to look at you before you begin talking.

Babies and Toddlers: Ages up to Two

How They Communicate

Crying is one of an infant's first ways of interacting through sound. By the time a baby is four weeks old, her cries are distinct. There are special cries for cravings, moisture, discomfort, and missing companionship. Within a couple of months, children also begin to coo and purr with satisfaction.

Between three to four months, children understand that when they make noise, people react. When a parent or health professional responds to a child's sobs, the baby starts to trust her methods of interaction, due to the fact that her requirements are being met. In the second six months of life, infants begin to babble in the language of their parents and other caregivers.

Young children and babies do not understand words out of context. Rather, they comprehend words in combination with your gestures, tone and face.

By eighteen to twenty-four months, kids begin to make use of activity words. These words share exactly what they wish or see, leaving out adjectives and other grammatical conventions. They may come out with brief phrases, such as "Mommy go" or "Foot wears on". Babies and kids also talk through gestures and intonation. What they do literally may be as important as what they actually point out.

Toddlers use words and smaller sentences to assert themselves. It is developmentally vital for a young child to claim these words.

Best Parenting Tips for Babies

Cuddle, touch, and croon to babies as a first form of interaction. When babies sob, you can assure them with your visibility and a comforting, relaxing tone. Children react to the feelings you are conveying rather than just what they see, feel, and listen to. They respond to your sadness, tension, happiness, or satisfaction.

Be mindful that tone and physical body language make a difference. In the same way, a soft and affectionate "Good evening" when you are tucking him in bed will comfort your kid by its soothing tone.

Stay physically linked is a method to connect. Infants like being close to their moms and dads. Holding them alongside your body provides peace of mind and comfort; a provider likewise permits you to move around and continue with your life.

When you are on the phone, do not be surprised if your baby cries. A baby knows when you are not paying attention, and he knows how to get that attention back. His wailing might come at an awkward time, but being aware of just what's triggering your child's reactions can help you remain patient and handle him when it happens.

Turn child talk into a two-way conversation. Encourage your child to make a pleasing flow of noises that at some point will lead to talking. Extend words and noises to help youngsters gain language abilities. If your kid says, "Go house," you could prolong his idea by saying, "You want to go our residence. We can leave in a couple of minutes."

Even if you are not sure just how much your child comprehends, talk anyhow! Like holding and kissing, words are an essential means of staying in contact with your infant. They will help your baby start to attach feelings and ideas to sounds.

Best Parenting Tips for Toddlers

When your toddler is between one and two years of age:

- Keep reading to your young child daily.
- Ask her to find items for you or name body components and items.
- Play matching games with your toddler.
- Motivate him to explore and attempt new points.
- Help to create your kid's language by chatting with her.
- Motivate your toddler's curiosity and capacity to acknowledge common objects by taking trips together on a bus or to the park.

Between two and three:

- Establish a unique time to check out manuals with your young child.
- Motivate your child to engage in pretend play.
- Play "Parade" or "Follow the Leader" with your toddler.
- Assist your youngster to explore her environments by taking her on a walk or wagon ride.
- Encourage your child to tell you his name and age.
- Teach your kid simple songs like "Twinkle, Twinkle, Little Star" or other childhood rhymes.

Pre-Schoolers: Ages Two to Five

How They Communicate

Between ages two and three, lots of pre-schoolers begin to make use of more difficult sentences. This does not mean that they recognize all of a grownup's words or abstract principles. Pre-schoolers are typically very literal thinkers and interpret ideas concretely. Many are just starting to think logically and recognize series of events.

Pre-schoolers know that they could use specific words to say just what they mean. They have actually long understood that their moms and dads' words have power over their lives, and they are starting to recognize that their own words can make a difference. They create a lot more effective meanings using their growing vocabulary.

"No" and "why" become common words for young pre-schoolers. "Why" is also a word a young child uses to doubt authority.

Young children like to participate in decisions. This offers them a feeling of control and self-reliance. A pre-schooler might believe, "I can take a different position from my mother—and I like it!" Or, "By demanding what I want, I am a big boy."

Pre-schoolers like to copy the words of others. They typically mimic remarks, expressions, and advanced statements. At times they abuse or overemphasize expressions, specifically during pretend play. A pre-schooler might say to a doll, "You are so bad you are going to jail for a hundred years!"

Young children like to hear about and describe the exact same occasion over and over. By paying attention and telling stories, young children begin to form viewpoints regarding the world and just how they fit into it.

Young children like to make up their very own descriptions. This helps them understand points they are just starting to comprehend. As an example, a pre-schooler might discuss her unhappiness about winter months by pointing out, "When the snow melts, the winter is sobbing." Young children may also embellish tales with wishful thinking.

Between the ages of three and five, pre-schoolers refine their understanding of the domino effect. Older young children understand basic explanations of cause and effect such as "The medicine will help you heal" or "If you consume healthy food, you will grow big and strong."

Young children likewise chat through their bodies, their play, and their art. Verbal communication still might not be the primary way many pre-schoolers know the world or share themselves.

Pre-schoolers need to say "no". For young children "no" is not always intended to start a power battle. It's simply an expression of self. "No, let me do it alone." "No, I do it." It is necessary to consider that your kid may merely be doing his job maturing and pointing out "yes" to himself rather than "no" to you.

Best Parenting Tips for Pre-Schoolers

Give your young child your complete attention. Also, a quick but intense interaction can meet your kid's need for communication. If she says, "Enjoy with me," and you are not readily available, you may clarify why or say, "I had a difficult day at the office today. I need three minutes to change. After that I can have fun with you." Pre-schoolers can understand your sensations and will certainly value your honesty.

Be aware of your tone. Because pre-schoolers are brand new to sentence-making themselves, they may have an increased understanding of your tone and physical body language.

Mirror your child's unspoken feelings. This helps put your kid's sensations into words. Enlist your pre-schooler's assistance in determining a trouble. For instance, you might say, "Did something in that motion picture scare you?" If your youngster doesn't reply, you might follow up by asking, "Could it have been the view of that character's face?"

Help your pre-schooler create psychological awareness. If there is misbehaviour, you can talk about it with each other. Most pre-schoolers can recognize a sentence like "Often I get angry too. It helps me to go into another room and take some deep breaths."

Offer restricted choices. Young children get a sense of command by making their own decisions. You might say, "Do you want to get dressed before or after breakfast today?"

Don't finish your sentence with "Okay?" unless you expect your kid to say "No". Asking your child if a task is okay can cause a prolonged discussion as well as a power struggle.

Grant a pre-schooler's desire in dreams. If your kid seems unhappy that a plaything has to be shared, you might point out, "Would you like it if you had the plaything all to yourself?"

Provide safe possibilities for young children to share their big feelings. As an example, if your child is remarkably upset, instead of saying, "Quit hollering," you might say, "Go into the washroom and scream as loud as you can for one minute."

Do not over-explain. Simple explanations may be much more effective than lengthy conversations. If your pre-schooler is having a tantrum, holding her close—or even just staying close by—may say more than any words you could speak.

If she says, "Play with me," and you are not readily available, you might describe why or state, "I had a tough day at work today." Pre-schoolers can recognize your feelings to a degree and will certainly value your sincerity.

School-Age Children: Ages Six to Eleven

How They Communicate

School-age little ones begin to view the world in complex ways. In this phase, youngsters typically move from being solid thinkers to being more reflective. They think even more logically about world events, while still seeing them subjectively. They begin to consider sources and start asking even tougher questions.

Between the ages of six and eleven little ones become purposeful. They think ahead of time about exactly what they want, and they frequently have a plan for the best way to get it. Because their communication pattern is impetuous and steered by their wishes, it could mask just how deep, wise, and loving they are within.

School-age kids at the same time feel dependent, resistant, or even rebellious toward their parents. School-age children may appear needy for days and then unexpectedly throw outbursts.

School-age children question, question, and criticize their moms and dads. They no longer consider their mother and father to be the sole authorities. This doubting is normal, and it indicates they are becoming essential thinkers. They may appear to distance themselves from, or even reject, individuals they adore a lot.

School-age children start to tailor their interaction methods to their environments. Younger children usually interact with a single style no matter where they are or who they are with. As school-age children spend more time away from home, they commonly establish new patterns of speaking based upon what their pals are saying out or what they listen to on television.

They may become private about their thoughts. No matter how positive a relationship a school-age child has with his mom and dad, he may now start to shut them out as his life outside the home starts to compete with his home life.

School-age kids develop a much more creative funny bone. They delight in telling puns and jokes and playing advanced games. They may recognize a lot more adult media and evaluate the rules and premises of the games they play.

School-age children are considerably more self-directed and peer-focused than when they were younger. Their behaviour and personality may seem to transform overnight. There is always a moment when you think, "I don't recognize this youngster." Then you realize, "Oh, she's just changing and growing up."

Best Parenting Tips for School-Age Children

Find time to talk. With a school-age child, you will not have as many possibilities for conversation as you did with your pre-schooler. As your youngster grows up, she may turn to you much less frequently, so you should make a special effort to hang around together.

Speak with your school-age child in a fully grown-up manner. School-age kids wish to have their "bigness" acknowledged. If they feel they are being talked to like infants (even if they happen to be behaving like them), they might be offended. You might state, "I expect you to begin your guide record. Just what time would you like to deal with it?" instead of "How many times do I have to tell you to do your book report?"

Show your school-age child respect. One way is to ask your kid for help in knowing her and her needs. If you acknowledge that your youngster has some information you do not have, she will understand that you respect her, even though you are making the final decisions.

Ask your school-age child specific rather than basic questions. As opposed to asking, "How was school?" you might ask, "Did your teacher discuss your science work?" Avoid leading questions. A query such as "Do you believe it's appropriate to talk to me like this?" often backfires. As an alternative, you might say, "I feel upset when you speak to me this way."

Listen to your school-age child without contradicting her. Rather than stating "That's ridiculous," you might simply say "Hmm" or "Truly." Ask specific questions based on the scenario your youngster has laid out.

Repeat what you heard your child state, but in a more mature way. You can reflect her statement through an inquiry. "Am I getting this right?" By saying this, you are respecting your kid's knowledge, making her feel understood, and urging her to tell you more. You might point out, "So, you believe your gym instructor is dumb, but you don't want me to step in? Can you tell me what you are upset about?"

Laugh a little and admit your blunders. At times, humour is the best method to fix a conflict, react to an upset, or make a request of your school-age child. You could also ask your kid for support in finding out what to do. Kids love to listen to moms and dads admit they were wrong. You might say, "Am I making a mess of this? Should we try to figure it out a different way?"

Ask your kid to aid establish her own limits. Do not hesitate to say "No" when your school-age kid (or you) needs it. Nonetheless, within reason, your child can set some guidelines as well. As an example, you could ask her to propose a sensible time to start her homework. "Discuss it and then back off." Ask your child to be in charge of determining what help is offered, exactly how much, and when (according to her teacher's instructions). This way you help your kid feel powerful in her own world.

If your school-age child won't talk to you, keep chatting anyway. You will certainly feel sometimes that you have lost your reliability with a school-age child. If you take silence or spontaneous opinions personally, things could go very terribly wrong. However, they are usually merely trying to establish their self-reliance.

Teen Years from Twelve to Eighteen

Every teen acts differently at this stage because lots of changes are taking place in their bodies and minds. Surroundings and school play a great role in their lives, so let's understand your teen child.

The teen years are a period of extreme development, not only physically but morally and intellectually. It's easy to see that it's a time of complication and revolution for numerous family members.

Despite some grownups' negative perceptions about adolescents, they are typically energetic, thoughtful, and utopian, with a deep passion for what is reasonable and ideal. So, although they can be a time of dispute between parents and children, the teen years are also a time to assist kids become the unique individuals they will certainly come to be.

Understanding the Teen Years

So when, specifically, do the teenage years start? The message to give your children is that everybody is different. There are early bloomers, late arrivals, quick developers, and slow-but-steady growers. In other words, there's a wide range of what is considered normal.

But it's important to make a (somewhat synthetic) distinction between adolescence and teenage years. Many of us think of adolescence as the development of adult sex-related attributes—busts, menstrual periods, pubic hair, and facial hair. These are certainly the most noticeable indications of adolescence and approaching adulthood, yet children who are showing physical changes (between the ages of eight and fourteen approximately) also can be going through a ton of changes that can't be conveniently seen from the exterior. These are the changes of the teenage years.

Lots of kids demonstrate the beginning of the teenage years with an impressive change in their behaviour around their moms and dads. They're beginning to separate from their mother and father and become much more independent. At the same time, kids this age are increasingly knowledgeable about how others, especially their peers, see them and are desperately trying to fit in. Their peers frequently become much more important than their parents in terms of making decisions.

Children usually start "trying on" various searches and identities, and they become really knowledgeable about how they differ from their peers, which can cause episodes of distress and conflict with parents.

Teens essentially communicate as grownups, with increasing maturity throughout high school. They understand abstract language, such as idioms and metaphors. Explanations might become more figurative and less literal.

Teenagers ought to be able to process texts and abstract meaning, relate word definitions and contexts, and know punctuation and intricate syntactic structures. However, communication is greater than the use and understanding of words; it additionally includes exactly how teens think of themselves, their peers, and authority figures.

As teens seek independence from family and develop their own identity, they begin thinking abstractly and become interested in moral issues. All of this influences the way they communicate and their belief system.

The message to deliver to your kid is that everyone is different.

Best Parenting Tips for the Teen Years

We have all heard moms and dads complaining about their teens. Your twelve-year-old was agreeable, enthusiastic, and eager to please. Your thirteen-year-old is defiant and irritable and seems determined to contradict every word you say.

If you're looking for a roadmap to discover how to deal with these years, below are some pointers:

- Read publications about teenagers.
- Reflect on your own teen years. Remember your struggles with pimples or your shame at developing early or late.
- Expect some state-of-mind modifications in your usually sunny youngster, and be prepared for more problems as she or he matures.

Moms and dads that know what's coming can handle it much better. And the more you know, the more you will be ready.

Here are a few tips to help you communicate with your teen:

- Make time during the day or evening to hear about your teen's activities. Be sure that they understand you are definitely interested and listening closely and meticulously.
- Remember to speak with your adolescent, not at him or her.
- Ask questions that go beyond "yes" or "no" answers to encourage further conversation.
- Take advantage of time spent on car journeys or standing in line at the grocery store to talk with your adolescent.

- Offer activities that supply chances to enhance interaction possibilities, such as being involved in or attending sporting and college events, playing games, and talking about current affairs.

And here are some tips to assist your adolescent in developing socially:

- Motivate your adolescent to take on new challenges.
- Talk with your teen about not losing sight of oneself in team situations.
- Encourage your teen to speak with a reputable grownup about troubles or worries, even if it is not you that he or she prefers to talk with.
- Discuss ways to manage and handle tension.
- Encourage opportunities to chat without making them feel strained.
- Use opportunities for talking, such as meals.
- Offer everyone the opportunity to discuss their day, including you.
- Help by clarifying any words or expressions that they do not recognize.
- Show that you are interested by making time to pay attention.

Teen years can be tough for many families. Young people might establish concepts, interests, and beliefs that are different to those of their moms and dads. This is part of the regular process of moving towards freedom. Moms and dads might struggle with just how much independence they ought to permit their children at various ages and in various conditions.

There is no prescription for this. Each teenager is different and really needs different insight. Communication with teenagers is different from connecting with younger children and can trigger problems and tensions.

If you follow some simple ideas, it may help to enhance interaction with your young adult. Always seek professional suggestions if you are concerned about your family relationships.

Problems That Can Affect Communication with Teenagers

The teenage years are a time of fast adjustment, not simply for the young adult but also for moms and dads as well. Often it might be tough to let go, but moms and dads should recognize that:

- A youngster's job is to mature and become an independent grownup. As a parent, you need to help young people through this process.
- Choices can now be made together. Try to review concerns to reach a result that you and your teen can both accept.
- Young people may have perspectives that are different from yours or might take part in activities that you don't understand. Attempt to see this as a benefit. They are learning to be their own person.
- You will always feel in charge of your kid's health and well-being no matter how old they are. When youngsters reach their adolescent years, they start to make their own choices. At times they make incorrect ones. Attempt to be supportive all the time. They will (hopefully) learn important lessons from their blunders.
- Throughout this time of constant change, both parents and kids need to take time to look after themselves.
- You have to show you value your teenagers and their originality. Show them your outright passion.

General Communication Tips with Teenagers

The most important thing is to keep the lines of communication open. Techniques include:

- Listen more than you talk. Remember that we are all offered two ears and one mouth. This tells us that we must invest twice as much time listening as talking. This is particularly important when talking with teenagers, who might tell us more if we give them the opportunity.

- Make time to spend together. Young adults are commonly busy with school, friends, and other interests, but you could have a chat with them over breakfast or supper. Offer to take them to or pick them up from places. This will give other possibilities for talks.
- Give them privacy. Teenagers require their own space. As an example, knock before you enter their room.
- Keep up with their passions. Pay attention to their popular music, view their television shows with them, and turn up to their sports practice sessions. Keep taking an energetic interest in their life.
- Be a loving parent. Adolescence is a time when youthful individuals frequently have a hard time with their changing feelings of identity and really need to feel enjoyed. Reassure them frequently. Celebrate their successes, forgive their blunders, listen closely to them when they have an issue, and show excitement about how they plan to fix it.
- Enjoy yourself. Make time for convenience and laughter. Good feelings help to create good connections.

Negative Communication with Teenagers

When people with different opinions live together, periodic skirmishes with your young adult are normal and are to be anticipated. Disagreement cannot be prevented. However, on-going disagreement can weaken the relationship between parents and a child.

Poor communication is a common reason for chronic disagreement. Examples of poor communication include nagging, harsh judgments, or tactics such as shouting to force compliance.

It's not always simple to acknowledge negative communication. Well-meaning moms and dads may be guilty of it because they desire their kid to attempt more difficult things. You are communicating negatively if any of the following are true.

- The discussion quickly degrades in to nagging, fighting, or screaming.
- You really feel mad, upset, denied, condemned, or unloved.
- The problem underlying the conflict never improves.

You can change negative communication into positive communication. Techniques include:

- Negotiate about how you communicate with each other. Exercise techniques to boost your communication. Brainstorm solutions together.
- Choose what it is necessary to argue over. A fundamental rule is that safety problems, such as not getting in in an automobile with a motorist who has been drinking, are always worth contesting. Other things, like cleaning up the unpleasant bedroom, may be easier to dismiss. Simply keep the door closed!
- Give positive criticism. Acknowledge and celebrate their achievements. When they have got things wrong, they do not really need to be reminded by you. They will understand themselves.
- Set a good example by apologizing when you're wrong.

You need to willingly give teenagers more freedom when they are ready to behave responsibly. For every right they gain, there is a responsibility that goes with it. Techniques include:

- Develop acceptable rules and regulations in consultation with your young adult. As an example, determine together on an appropriate curfew for weekend evenings.
- When working out house rules with teenagers, be prepared to take risks. Try to give ground on the least important concerns.

- Stop and consider before you say no to a request. Is your teenager now old enough or sufficiently accountable for you to say yes this time?
- If you do say no, explain why. Remember, saying "because I said so" is simply asking for a fight! Give good reasons, such as using the safety argument.
- Help them to take responsibility for themselves. Talk about issues such as drink spiking or protected sex. Browse the better health stations for good information. Read through the fact sheets with each other and talk about any concerns you both might have.

Listen more and talk less. Take the time to listen. You may be surprised how much teenagers will confide in you if they feel they are really being listened to. Techniques include:

- When they speak to you, truly listen closely. Stop what you're doing, look them in the eye, and don t interrupt.
- Avoid angry or impatient body movement. As an example, don't rolls your eyes or sigh.
- Cherish that your young adult has a different world view. Address them as you would a friend and respect their point of view. They may have quite well-thought-through opinions that are simply different to yours.
- Use "I" statements instead of "you" statements. For instance, don't say, "You're so tactless; you never ever inform me where you're going." Rather, say, "If I don't understand where you are, I fret about you."
- Avoid sarcasm, criticism, and shouting.
- Don t make assumptions or try to mind read. Listen.
- Young people will certainly stop talking if you refuse to listen pleasantly.

Some Tips on How to Get Your Kid Talking

You would certainly like to know exactly what your kid did in school today, but all she'll state is "absolutely nothing". What is the key to getting her to open up? Everyone really needs a chance to capture their breath at the end of the day. Sure, some children babble away when they get home, but the majority are exhausted and really need a break. Offer your youngster one, let her recover, and then try these ideas:

- Be specific.
- Ask additional targeted questions. "Did you choose a brand new story from the guide bin today? Which one did you pick?" or "What computer games did you play in recreation today?"
- Try not to browbeat her.
- When she states, "I didn't manage to use the monkey bars today," avoid launching into an inquisition. Simply react with "The monkey bars?" She understands you're listening. After that, allow her continue.
- Acknowledge her feelings.
- Just saying "I see you're thrilled about something" or "You seem awfully tired today" may offer her the springboard she needs to tell you about her day.
- Keep it casual.
- Many kids find it easier to chat when your attention isn't really concentrated just on their words, so converse informally while you make dinner or walk the puppy with each other.

Do not overlook the importance of this chapter. It would make me happy if you were so enthusiastic about its contents that you reread it before proceeding to the next one. Remember, better communication with your child will create a strong bond between you and your child.

Chapter 4:

BEHAVIOUR

Moms and dads frequently have difficulty telling the difference between variations in regular behaviour and true behavioural problems. In reality, the difference between abnormal and typical habits is not absolute; usually it refers to level or our assumptions. A line often separates typical from abnormal behaviour, in part due to the fact that exactly what is "typical" depends upon the child's level of advancement, which can differ significantly amongst children of the same age. Development can be uneven too, with a child's social development lagging behind his intellectual growth, or the other way around. Additionally, "normal" habits are in part determined by the context in which things happen—that is, by the particular situation and time and by the youngster's own family members' assumptions and social and cultural background.

Understanding your kid's special developmental improvement is necessary in order to interpret, accept, or adjust his behaviour (as well as your own). Bear in mind that children have enormous individual variations of temperament, habits, and development.

Three Types of Behaviour

Some parents find it helpful to consider three general kinds of behaviour:

- Some kinds of behaviour are wanted and approved. They might consist of doing homework, being courteous, and doing chores. These actions obtain compliments freely and effortlessly.
- Other behaviour is not sanctioned but is allowed under certain conditions, such as during times of illness (of a child or a mom or a dad) or anxiety (a move, for example,

or the birth of a brand new brother or sister). These sorts of habits might consist of ignoring chores, regressive behaviour (such as baby talk), or being exceedingly self-centred.

- Still other sorts of habits cannot and should not be put up with or reinforced. They include activities that are unsafe to the physical, emotional, or social health of the youngster, the relative, or others. They might hamper the child's intellectual advancement. They may be forbidden by legislation, principles, faith, or social mores. They might include really aggressive or damaging habits, overt bigotry or prejudice, stealing, cigarette smoking, failing college, or an intense brother or sister rivalry.

Typical behaviour in children depends upon the child's age, personality, and physical and emotional advancement. A kid's behaviour may be an issue if it doesn't match the assumptions of the family members or if it is disruptive. Typical or "excellent" habits are usually identified by whether they are socially, culturally, and developmentally proper. Understanding exactly what to expect from your child at each age will help you decide whether his or her habits are normal.

Children go through unique periods of advancement as they move from babies to young adults. During each of these phases, several changes in the development of the mind are taking place. When these developments take place is genetically determined— exactly what develops and roughly when. Environmental factors and interactions with key people within that atmosphere have significant influence on how each child advances from each developing occasion.

"Ages and Stages" is a term used to lay out general crucial periods in the human development timeline. Throughout each phase, growth and development take place in the key developmental areas, including physical, intellectual, linguistic, and socio-psychological. Our objective is to help moms and dads know exactly what is occurring in their child's brain and body during each stage in the hope that they will be able to offer the required support, reassurance, framework and interventions to enable a kid to advance through each stage as easily and successfully as possible based upon each youngster's unique set of characteristics and interests.

Why Children Misbehave

When you consult a professional person or get in touch with friends and family concerning difficulties you have with your kids, you will be given a great deal of recommendations. Sometimes this assistance is disturbing, since it makes you really feel bad or because people contradict each other. It can be really complicated.

It becomes more complicated when you ask people why your children behave in the way they do. Commonly, children might misbehave due to family difficulties, such as bereavement, illness, breakup, remarriage, or school issues, such as bullying, lack of confidence, troubles with friends or siblings, and such like. Even if this is the case, you may find this information valuable. It is useful to think of bad habits as an indication that something is wrong. If you think about it, most people want to be liked and helped, not to stay mad, separated, and hurt.

Whatever the causes of bad behaviour may be, try to get in touch with your kid concerning their psychological grief and feelings. It is often more useful to guess how a youngster is feeling than to ask them. For instance, you can say, "I guess you're angry (or upset or in pain) about something, which is why you are acting this way." This can help the child to open up much more, believing you recognize and connect with their feelings. You will often find that if you ask a youngster exactly how they are really feeling, they get confused or merely refuse to tell you. Enlisting the aid of your partner, family member, good friend, or educator can make it less complicated for your youngster to talk. At times, a professional counsellor with experience of speaking with youngsters could help also.

Don't confuse getting in touch with sorting it all out. Occasionally it can be the same, but you will be fortunate if this happens by itself. Often kids decline to chat as a way of showing exactly how they feel and refuse to talk with you no matter how approachable you might be towards them.

Youngsters who are really raunchy, assertive, or bold commonly feel out of control. When uncontrollable youngsters discuss exactly how they really feel, they commonly share just how frightening it is to be this way. They want to get better control of their feelings or for someone else to help them control them. Children who run out of control commonly feel harmful, sad, upset, and helpless. They may really feel separated and lonely. When you encounter a cheeky and defiant child, this might be difficult to believe.

When you go to an expert or talk to friends and family members about troubles you are having with your youngsters, you will certainly be offered a whole lot of recommendations. It becomes a lot more complicated when you ask people why your child or children act in the ways they do. At times kids decline to talk as a means of expressing exactly how they feel and decline to chat to you however reasonable you might be to them.

What Can I Do to Change My Child's Behaviour?

Children often continue a habit when it is rewarded and quit a habit when it is ignored. Consistency in your response to behaviour is important, because rewarding and punishing the same behaviour at different times puzzles your youngster. When you believe your child's behaviour may be a trouble, you have three choices.

- Determine that the habits are not an issue because they are appropriate to the kid's age and stage of development.
- Attempt to stop the behaviour, either by ignoring it or by punishing it.

- Introduce a new behaviour that you prefer and strengthen it by rewarding your child.

How do I stop misbehaviour?

The very best means to stop unwanted habits is to ignore them. This method works best over a period of time. When you want the behaviour to stop promptly, you could utilize the time-out method.

How Do I Use the Time-Out Method?

Determine in advance the behaviours that will cause a time-out (usually outbursts or harmful or vigorous habits). Decide on a time-out place that is uninteresting for the kid and not frightening, such as a playpen, chair, or corner. When you're far from home, consider making use of an automobile or a nearby seating area as a time-out location.

When the inappropriate behaviour occurs, inform the child it is unacceptable and offer a caution that you will certainly put him or her in time-out if the behaviour does not stop. Stay calm and do not look upset. If your child goes on misbehaving, gently take him or her to the time-out location.

Ideally, take note of just how long your child has been on break. Set a timer so your youngster will understand when time-out is over. The break needs to be brief (usually one minute for each year old) and should begin promptly after getting to the time-out place or after the child relaxes. You need to remain within view or earshot of the child, but don't speak to him or her. Gently return the youngster to the location and consider recasting the timer if he or she leaves the time-out area. When the break is over, allow the kid leave the time-out location. Do not review the bad behaviour, but instead seek methods to reward and improve good behaviour later.

How Do I Encourage a New Desired Behaviour?

One method to encourage good habits is to use an incentive system. Kids who find out that bad habits are not tolerated and that good behaviour is rewarded are discovering skills that will last them a lifetime.

Select one or two habits you would wish to change (for instance, bedtime routines, tooth cleaning, or picking up toys). Select a reward your child would appreciate. Useful examples might include an additional bedtime story, putting off bedtime by half an hour, a favourite snack, or, for older children, earning points toward a unique plaything, a benefit, or a small amount of money.

Discuss the wanted behaviour and the benefit to the child. "If you get into your pyjamas and brush your teeth before this television show is over, you can stay up a half hour later." Ask just once. Give the benefit if the kid does what you ask. You can help the kid if necessary, but don't get too involved. Any sort of attention from moms and dads, including negative attention, is satisfying to youngsters. They may be happy to have adult attention as an alternative to the reward! Warning statements, such as "In five minutes, playtime will be over" are useful when you are teaching your child brand new behaviours.

This system helps you avoid power struggles with your youngster. Nonetheless, your kid is not punished if he or she chooses not to act as you ask; he or she just does not obtain the benefit.

Some Good Ways to Reward Your Child

Beat the Time Clock. (This is an excellent technique for a dawdling kid.) Ask the kid to do a task. Set a timer. If the task is done before the timer rings, your youngster obtains a reward. To decide the amount of time to allow the kid, figure out your kid's "best time" to do that task and add five minutes.

The Good Behaviour Game. (This is great for teaching brand new habits.) Compose a short list of good behaviours on a graph and mark the chart with a star each time you see the good behaviour. After your child has earned a small number of stars (depending upon the kid's age), offer your kid a reward.

Good Marks/Bad Marks. (This is the finest method for difficult, highly active kids.) Quickly put a mark on a chart or on your child's hand each time you see him or her behaving well. As an example, if you see your child playing quietly, fixing an issue without fighting, getting playthings, or checking out a publication, you would certainly mark the graph. After a specific number of marks, offer your youngster an incentive. You can also make adverse marks each time a bad habit is developed. If you do this, just give your child a reward if there are more good marks than adverse marks.

Quiet Time. (This is extremely useful when you're making dinner.) Ask your kid to play quietly alone or with a sibling for w while (maybe thirty minutes). Review your child frequently (every two to five minutes, depending on the child's age) and offer an incentive or a token for each and every few times they are quiet or playing well. Progressively extend the periods; go from inspecting your child's behaviour every two to five minutes to checking every thirty minutes, but continuously provide incentives for each and every time period your kid has been quiet or played well.

What Else Can I Do to Help My Child Behave Well?

Make a list of essential rules and go over them with your child. Avoid power struggles, no-win situations, and extremes. When you think you've overreacted, it's much better to make use of good sense to fix the problem, even if you have to be inconsistent with your reward or punishment approach. Avoid doing this too often as it could confuse your kid.

Accept your youngster's basic character, whether it's reluctant, social, energetic, or talkative. Fundamental personality can be changed a little, but not very much. Try to stay away from scenarios that could make your youngster cranky by making him or her overly stimulated, tired, or worn out. Do not criticize your youngster in front of other people. Explain your youngster's behaviour as bad, but don't label your child as bad. When he or she deserves it, regularly praise your youngster. Touch him or her affectionately and frequently. Kids want and really need attention from their moms and dads.

Establish little regimens and routines, particularly at bedtimes and mealtimes. Give warning statements, such as "In five minutes, we'll be eating dinner." Allow your child to make choices whenever feasible. For instance, you can ask, "Do you wish to wear your red pyjamas or your blue pyjamas to bed tonight?"

As children age, they may take pleasure in becoming involved in making household guidelines. Don't discuss the rules at the time of the misbehaviour, but welcome your child to participate in making new regulations on a later occasion. Avoid doing this too often as it may confuse your child.

Changing Your Own Behaviour

As you check out the suggestions in this guide, you might think, "Seems fantastic. That will actually work for me." Reviewing a new strategy is not the same as engaging in a brand-new method. Exercising originality requires changing your own behaviour. Any modification in behaviour implies transforming routines. Practices are not easy to transform. Old practices are comfortable, new ones are not.

As you proceed through this book, you will be learning about effective mom and dad behaviours. You will be reading about strategies and techniques that you should make use of even more. You will find out about parent habits that are counter-productive. You should engage in doing these behaviours less. You will also discover that several of your present concepts are appropriate and need no change. As you check out, make a list of behaviours that you should practice much more, habits you have to practice much less, and habits that are appropriate and should be introduced.

Because it takes about a month to develop brand new practices, assess your checklist two or three times a week for the next four weeks. This evaluation will help you confirm your brand new practices more quickly.

Before proceeding to the next chapter, pause a while and reflect over this one. If it has not excited you, if it has not caused you to overflow with enthusiasm, you have missed a point or two and should reread part or all of it.

Chapter 5:

RULES

Establishing House Rules for Teenagers

Parenting grows a lot tougher than ever before as soon as little ones hit the adolescent years. Normal teenage habits naturally include disobedience, and there is the possibility of even more severe behaviour problems. Even with their wish to be independent, young adults need rules and regulations to help them prepare for real life.

Parenting young adults requires a delicate balance between providing them sufficient assistance to ensure they are making healthy selections while also allowing them sufficient independence to make errors. Set up rules and regulations that appreciate your young adult's need to be independent while also ensuring they are behaving responsibly. When a policy gets broken, clearly summarize what negative consequences will be in store.

Young adults still really need the very same five types of guidelines as younger kids. When setting up house rules for your young adult, develop stricter rules in the areas where your teen still needs the most support. When teens have a hard time complying with the rules, it is an indication that they aren't all set for that much responsibility yet and may really need more guidance. As your young adult shows he can adhere to the rules, allow for better self-reliance.

Rules that Promote Safety

Teenagers tend to believe they are immortal. They likewise often are impetuous, which is why it is essential to set policies that promote safety.

Driving. Auto accidents are the top killer of teens. Teens need clear regulations about driving privileges and safety. Give them policies to minimize distractions by setting limitations on smart phone usage in the automobile and by providing clear guidelines about passengers. Establish regulations about speeding and make it clear exactly what will certainly take place if any sort of safety violations happen.

Drugs and Alcoholic Beverages. Teenagers have to be informed about the realities of drug and alcohol use. If they are caught experimenting with drugs, talk about exactly how to make good choices and established definite repercussions about exactly what will happen. Talk about exactly how they could get out of a situation if they are at an event or if they need a trip home.

Curfew. When it comes to young adults, it's not to be expected that anything wonderful is going to take place during the late evening and overnight hours. Set a certain curfew time, and if your teenager reveals responsibility in recognizing an early curfew, consider making the curfew later.

Rules That Teach Morality

The adolescent years provide you a chance to actually inspire values. It's important to model the behaviour that you wish to see so that you do not come across as a hypocrite. Pick the most essential values that you intend to impart in your teen and establish some guidelines that address those morals. Although these regulations will be specific to your family members, there are a few areas that numerous families can agree on.

Honesty. Set policies with your young child that promote honesty. If your young adult tries to lie to cover up his tracks, agree that consequences for misbehaviour will certainly be a lot more serious. Also consider policies that prevent dishonesty on homework.

Treating Others Respectfully. Teenagers often really need guidelines that motivate them to deal with others respectfully. Policies about gossiping, bullying, and not arguing can be vital components.

Rules That Encourage Healthy Habits

Most young adults aren't well known for their motivation. They usually need help from an adult to create healthy and balanced behaviours that determine how they spend their time and care for themselves.

Job. Homework, jobs, and part-time work often aren't at the top of a teen's to-do list. They may require rules that guarantee they get their work done. Setting up a time to do homework or connecting benefits to chores and motivating your teenager to make spending money with a part-time job could encourage good habits.

Leisure. Young adults often really need policies to help them spend their extra time purposefully. Set limitations on the use of electronic devices so your adolescent's spare waking hours are not devoted to the computer system, cellular phone, or video games. Likewise, be clear about where your young adult is allowed to hang out.

Self-Care. Although the majority of teenagers do not need suggestions to clean their teeth, they do still tend to really need help with self-care. Take into consideration policies to promote healthy and balanced eating, excellent sleeping habits, workouts, and good health.

Rules That Prepare Teenagers for the Real World

The adolescent years offer a brief window of time for your kid to get ready for the real world. Check out your teen's habits and consider just what else your teen must find out before he's ready to live on his own. Provide discipline that shows some life capabilities necessary for the real world which are given below.

Cash. Educate your child about the best ways to take care of cash so he is ready for budgeting in the real world. Set regulations concerning the amount of money he has to save and help him make good choices with his spending habits. Show him ways to plan a budget and identify what sorts of things he should buy with his own money.

Self-Control. Teenagers really need self-discipline so they can live on their own. When suitable, establish rules that grant some liberty and allows for natural effects.

Rules That Enhance Social Skills

Young adults often require major adjustments in the social skills area. Establish rules that help your young adult discover and engage in healthy and balanced ways to manage his emotional states and interact with other people.

Friends. The sort of friends your kid decides on is likely to have a large effect on his behaviour. Set limitations on exactly how much time they can spend together outside of college if your young adult decides on friends who cause difficulties. Teens likewise usually need adult assistance about ways to deal with issues such as bullying and disagreements with their friends.

Dating. Set up regulations concerning dating that provide your young adult some self-reliance but likewise ensure that your teenager is being safe. Set clear guidelines regarding the sorts of behaviour that is allowed and how much contact is acceptable.

Emotional Skills. Teenagers have a natural tendency to be emotional. When he's angry, rules that promote teenager administration are particularly crucial if you've got a teenager who breaks rules or makes threats. Teach analytical skills to teach safe and effective ways to fix problems independently.

How about rereading this chapter before starting the next one?

Chapter 6:

CHILD SAFETY FIRST

Child Safety First: The First Year

When a child enters your family, it is time to ensure that your residence is a safe place. Look over your home for points that could be hazardous to your baby. As a mom or dad, it is your job to ensure that you provide a secure home for your infant. It likewise is essential that you take the necessary actions to see to it that you are mentally prepared for your new baby. Here are a few tips to keep your child safe.

- Do not shake your infant—ever! Infants have extremely weak neck muscles that are not yet able to support their heads. If you shake your baby, you can damage his brain and even cause his death.
- Ensure you always place your infant to sleep on her spine to avoid sudden infant death syndrome (often called SIDS). Review even more about new referrals for risk-free rest for babies below.
- Protect your child and family members from second-hand smoke. Do not allow anyone to smoke in your home.
- Place your baby in a rear-facing safety seat in the back seat while he is riding in a car.
- Prevent your child from choking by dividing her food into little morsels. Do not allow her to play with small toys or various other items that might be easy for her to ingest.
- Don't let your child play with anything that might cover her face.
- Never carry warm liquids or foods near your child or while you are holding him.
- Vaccinations are necessary to secure your youngster's health and safety. It is crucial that your kid gets the right shots at the proper time since children can get major

diseases. Talk with your child's medical professional to ensure that your child is current on her vaccinations.

Child Safety First: Ages One and Two

Because your child is moving around more, he will certainly come across additional hazards. Hazardous circumstances can occur quickly, so keep a close eye on your youngster. Here are a few pointers to help keep your growing kid secure.

- Do *not* leave your kid near or around water (for example, bath tubs, pools, lakes, whirlpools, or the ocean) without a person watching her. Fence off yard swimming pools. Drowning is the leading reason for trauma and death amongst this age group.
- Block off stairs with a little gate or fence. Lock doors to harmful places such as the garage or basement.
- Ensure that your home is toddler-proof by placing plug covers on all unused electric outlets.
- Keep kitchen area appliances, irons, and heating units out of reach of your kid. Turn pot takes care of toward the rear of the stove.
- Keep sharp objects such as scissors, knives, and pencils in a safe place.
- Secure medicines, household cleaning products, and toxins.
- Do *not* leave your young child alone in any kind of vehicle even for a few minutes.
- Store any sort of firearms in a place safe from his reach.
- Keep your child's safety seat rear-facing as long as possible. According to the National Freeway Quality Traffic Safety Management it's the most effective method to keep her secure. Your kid should remain in a rear-facing car seat until she reaches the top height or weight restriction allowed by the safety seat's manufacturer. As soon as your child outgrows the rear-facing car seat, she is ready to take a trip in a forward-facing safety seat with a harness.

Child Safety First: Ages Two and Three

Now that your kid is moving a lot more, he will certainly also discover more dangers. Hazardous scenarios can occur quickly, so keep a close eye on your kid. Here are a few pointers to help keep your growing toddler protected.

- Do *not* leave your kid near or around water (for example, bath tubs, pools, lakes, whirlpools, or the ocean) without a person watching her. Fence off yard swimming pools. Drowning is the leading reason for trauma and death amongst this age group.
- Urge your young child to sit while eating and to chew his meals thoroughly to prevent choking.
- Check playthings routinely for loose or damaged parts.
- Urge your kid not to place pencils or crayons in her mouth when colouring or drawing.
- Do *not* hold hot drinks while your child is sitting on your lap. Sudden movements can create a spill and might lead to your kid being burned.
- See to it that your youngster sits in the back seat and is buckled up appropriately in a safety seat with a harness.

Child Safety First: Ages Three to Five

As your youngster starts to become a lot more independent and spends more time outdoors, it is very important that you and your youngster are aware of methods to stay safe. Here are a couple of suggestions to protect your kid.

- Tell your kid why it is important to stay out of traffic. Tell him not to play in the road or run after lost balls.
- When permitting your kid use her tricycle, be careful. Keep her on the walkway and away from traffic, and always have her wear a helmet.
- Inspect outdoor playground equipment. Make certain there are no loose parts or sharp edges.

- Watch your child at all times, especially when he is playing outside.
- Be safe in the water. Teach your child to dive, but monitor her at all times when she is in or around any physical body of water (including kiddie pools).
- Instruct your child the best ways to be protected around strangers.
- Keep your kid in a forward-facing car seat with a harness up until he reaches the top height or weight limitation allowed by the safety seat's manufacturer. When your child grows out of the forward-facing safety seat with a harness, it will be time for him to move to a booster seat, but still in the rear of the automobile. The National Highway Traffic Safety Administration has information on how to keep your child safe while riding in a vehicle.

Child Safety First: Ages Six to Eight

A lot more physical potential and even more independence can put youngsters at risk for traumas from falls and collisions. Motor vehicle collisions are the most typical cause of unintentional injury among kids this age.

- Protect your kid appropriately in the automobile. For details, browse through the American Academy of Paediatrics' *Car Safety Seats: A Guide for Families.*
- Teach your youngster to look out for traffic and how to be safe when walking to school, using a bike, and playing outside.
- Make certain your youngster understands water safety, and always supervise her when she's swimming or having fun near water.
- Supervise your child when he's participating in risky activities, such as climbing.
- When she requires it, talk with your child concerning how to ask for help.
- Keep potentially hazardous household items, tools, equipment, and firearms out of your youngster's reach.

Child Safety First: Ages Nine to Eleven

Additional independence and less grownup supervision can put children in danger of injuries from falls and other accidents. Here are a few suggestions to aid secure your kid.

- Safeguard your child in the car. The National Highway Traffic Safety Administration recommends that you keep your youngster in a car seat up until he is big enough to wear a seat belt properly. Remember, your youngster ought to still use in the back seat until he or she is twelve years of age, since it's more secure there. Motor vehicle accidents are the most common cause of death by unintentional injury among children of this age.
- Know where your youngster is and whether a reliable grownup is present. Make plans with your child for when he will be certain to call you, where you can find him, and exactly what time you expect him home.
- Make sure your kid uses a helmet when riding a skateboard or a bike, using inline skates, riding on a motorcycle, snowmobile, or all-terrain vehicle, or playing contact sports.
- Many children get home from school before their moms and dads get home from work. It is important to have certain guidelines and plans for your child when she is home alone.

Child Safety First: Ages Twelve to Fourteen

You play a vital part in keeping your kid secure, no matter how old they are. Below are a couple of pointers to safeguard your child.

- Ensure your teen understands the importance of wearing seatbelts. Automobile crashes are the leading cause of death among twelve- to fourteen-year-olds.
- Urge your teenager to put on a helmet when riding a skateboard or a bike or using inline skates, using a

motorcycle, snow sled, or all-terrain vehicle, or playing contact sports. Injuries from sporting activities and similar pursuits are common.

- Talk with your teen about the dangers of drugs, drinking, cigarettes, and high-risk sexual activity. Ask him what he believes and understands about these issues, and share your thoughts and feelings with him. Pay attention to what he says and address his inquiries honestly and directly.
- Talk with your teen about the importance of having good friends who are interested in positive activities. Motivate her to avoid peers who pressure her to make unhealthy choices.
- Know where your teen is and whether a grownup is present. Make plans with him for when he will be certain to call you, where you can find him, and what time you expect him home.
- Set clear regulations for your adolescent when she is home alone. Talk about such issues as having friends at the house, how to manage situations that can be harmful (emergency situations, fire, drugs, sex, etc.), and completing homework or household chores.

Child Safety First: Ages Fifteen to Seventeen

You play a vital job in keeping your child secure, regardless of just how old they are. Here are a few ways to help safeguard your child.

- Talk with your teen about the dangers of driving and how to be safe while driving. You can keep your adolescent on the right track. Automobile collisions are the leading cause of unintentional injury among teens, but few teenagers take measures to minimize their risk of injury.
- Advise your adolescent to use a helmet when riding a bike, motorbike, or all-terrain vehicle. Unintended traumas resulting from involvement in sports and various other activities are common.

- Talk with your teen about suicide and focus on warning signs. Suicide is the third leading cause of death amongst youth fifteen through twenty-four years of age.
- Talk with your teen about the risks of drugs, consuming alcohol, cigarette smoking, and dangerous sex. Ask him exactly what he thinks and knows regarding these problems, and share your feelings with him. Hear just what he says and answer his questions honestly and straightforwardly.
- Talk with your teenager about the importance of selecting friends who do not behave in unhealthy or harmful ways.
- Know where your teen is and whether a grownup is present. Make plans with him for when he will be certain to call you, where you can find him, and what time you expect him home.

Top Internet Safety Tips for Parents

While no technology is fail-safe, use parent controls do add another layer of security. The key is to see to it that you have something that mirrors your values and offers technical support, rather than attempting to take control in your role as a mom or dad. Just ask yourself, what's your primary objective?

It's a given that we generally know where our little ones are every single day, whom they're with, and exactly what they're doing. In the electronic world, where even our youngest kids are spending a growing amount of time, we're often reduced to the role of spectator, and many of us are reeling from a situation of electronic whiplash. Our kids might very well comprehend today's modern technology much better than we do.

Little ones today have only known a world that's cyber-filled, and innovation is woven into every aspect of their lives. It informs their relationships, their education and learning, and even their understanding of the world. We're rushing to figure out which regulations to set and how to enforce them.

The difficulty is that this specific topic isn't covered in the parental playbook. That chapter hasn't been composed yet, and culture hasn't yet had time to come up with requirements.

We have a legal age and a driving age, yet there's no solid conventional wisdom about exactly what age kids can securely browse the web alone or text a friend on their cell phone, or about what our duty as moms and dads should be in keeping tabs on our tykes.

The Internet can be a remarkable resource for children. They can use it to study their school work, interact with teachers and various other kids, and play interactive games. Children who are old enough to type a couple of letters on the keyboard could literally access the world.

However that increased access could also pose threats. An eight-year-old might do an on-line search for "Lego". With just one missed keystroke, the word "legs" is typed instead, and the kid may be routed to a variety of websites with an emphasis on legs—some of which could contain adult material.

That's why it's important to be aware of exactly what your little ones see and listen to on the net, who they meet, and just what they share about themselves online.

Just like any other protection issue, it's wise to chat with your kids concerning your worries, benefit from sources to safeguard them, and keep a close eye on their activities.

A federal law, the Children's Online Privacy Protection Act (COPPA), was created to help protect kids online. It's designed to keep anyone from obtaining a child's personal information without a parent knowing about it and agreeing to it first.

COPPA requires websites to explain their privacy policies on the site and get parental consent before collecting or using a child's personal information, such as a name, address, phone number, or Social Security number.

The law also prohibits a site from requiring a child to provide more personal information than necessary to play a game or participate in a contest.

But even with this law, your kids' best online protection is you. By talking to them about potential online dangers and monitoring their computer use, you'll help them surf the Internet safely.

Talk with your child about Web security as soon as he or she begins using the Web. It is never too early to start going over the importance of being a good electronic citizen.

Use an age-appropriate filtering system that oversees and shuts out software on all Internet-enabled devices used by your kid, including laptop computers, cordless phones, and computer games.

Remain associated with your child's online world by setting limits on his or her "screen time" and monitoring whom your child is connecting with online.

Learn more about the websites your kid is visiting, and educate yourself about your child's activities on the Internet. Review FOSI's *Internet Safety Deal* with your relatives, and think about having all family members sign the contract.

Explain to your youngster that he must never give out individually identifiable information online. For instance, your kid ought to know that he needs to not publish detailed information concerning his whereabouts.

See to it that your child understands never to meet with somebody they met online in person without initially talking with you about the situation.

Tell your youngster to never share their passwords with anybody, including friends.

Describe the repercussions of uploading unacceptable material online. For example, a youngster's reputation can be impacted by a posting or a photo that is shared.

Monitor your youngster's cell phone usage and review text messages sent out and received, including images downloaded and uploaded.

Educate yourself on the current dangers facing children online (e.g., cyber bullying, sexting, and so on) and arm yourself with details that will allow you to speak with your youngster about being a good electronic citizen.

To get the most good from this book, you should reread the chapters again.

Chapter 7:

OVERCOMING LAZINESS IN CHILDREN

Sluggish little ones might come from sluggish moms and dads who intend to be pals with their kids and don't give them the appropriate self-control a child really needs on an everyday basis.

Have you heard your little ones saying any of the following?

"I'll do it later . . ."

"I don't have time to do it now . . ."

"I'll do it when I wake up in the morning . . ."

"I'll do it in the late night before I go to sleep . . ."

"I'll do it as soon as I get home . . ."

There is nothing more annoying than trying to motivate an uninspired kid, especially when absolutely nothing works. You lecture them relentlessly about the future and how vital it is to do well in college, but try as you may, their efficiency doesn't improve. Just what do you do? This chapter offers some suggestions.

Health Problems. While some children are intrinsically much more energetic compared to others, most little ones are not normally lazy. If your kid seems to be tired and indifferent, this could be for a couple of reasons.

As kids grow, their bodies need to rest more than usual. If your kid is having a brand new attack of apparent laziness, give it a little time and allow his body to grow. As soon as his body catches up, he may be back to normal.

If you suspect any health care issues are causing laziness, have your child assessed by a paediatrician to eliminate any kind of physical problem.

Short-Term Goals and Rewards. Do not slam your youngster, but help her find ways to do well. With my son, money is not a motivation, so we make up a sticker chart weekly. If he gets his homework done and keeps his bed made, we mark a "day". Considering that we have other children, this is typically something as straightforward as a stroll without the various other kids, or a trip to the store for some sweets.

Find the thing that will steer your kids to be successful, and afterwards build it into their lives as a goal.

Stickers suffice for smaller kids, but as they get older, make sure to keep the rewards something you can follow through on.

Praise. Even if your youngster doesn't achieve every target you have set, lavish him with appreciation for the things he did well. Mention how his individual effort equates to success.

Praise your youngster with words that point out their initiative being the reason for meeting the targets. This will help them recognize their part in success.

Just Keep a Positive Attitude. As a parent, you establish the tone for your child's education and life choices. If you perceive university as fun and valuable, it's likely your kids will do the same.

If they see you criticizing, it's going to help them justify activities that are negative towards school.

Time Management. This has actually been a real battle for my child who ignores time and target dates. He is so quiet that I usually don't realize that he isn't doing what I asked.

We have actually developed a chart with what he needs to be doing at particular times in the day, and I have to follow through with helping him achieve it.

This is definitely important for survival in the real world, so make sure you discover ways to help your children get over laziness and handle their time.

Encourage Your Children's Interests. For a kid who would never read through and was always lazy, I was surprised to find that this little boy was interested in trains. He had actually remembered the entire train timetable, including arrival and departure times, the names of the stations, the different type of engines, and so on.

If you can locate your kid's particular niche and feed it, learning will certainly become incidental. This is sometimes a lot more difficult in a classroom setting, but if you communicate your child's interest to his teachers, they can coax performance out of him.

Extracurricular Activities. Whether you select this as part of the rewards/short-term goals or not is up to you, however sometimes your kid will flourish if they are offered an outlet to reveal their ingenuity.

You should motivate your youngster with imaginative means to find their passion. That skill is simply waiting to come out.

Involve them in team or personal tasks that make them satisfied. Just like us grownups, when we are happy, every part of our life is improved.

Adjust Your Expectations. If you are having a tough time accepting your kid's seeming lack of motivation, embrace it. There are some kids who are just artsy, poetic dreamers, and they could bring joy in to your lives in ways you never would have thought of.

Spend extra time learning and encouraging your little ones, because they will certainly be the ones that come back for the holidays every year. Understanding their interests will deliver joy to you and to them for your entire lives.

You are free to appreciate them once you discover and accept that there are some kids who won't be encouraged to be exactly how you feel they should be.

Keep an Open Relationship with Your Child That Is Respectful and Positive. Do not allow them to remain on his or her own situation or problems. You have to show them that you are on their team and work with them, not against them.

Use the "when you" policy. Do not permit them to do things they enjoy until after they have completed their assignments, tasks, study, or homework. This will give them something to pursue and provide some inspiration.

Do not wait for everything to get out of control. At the first indicator of grades dropping, that is your cue to involve yourself in getting your child back on track.

Ask the Instructor. Sit down with your youngster's teacher and together make a strategy to help your youngster get on track and remain on track. Team effort can help get the job done.

Designate a Study Spot. Some children function most effectively in silent spots, while others do better with turmoil around them. Try having your child work in different atmospheres until you locate the one that works best for them.

Break It Down. If your youngster really feels overloaded, particularly with large tasks, help them break it down in to little chunks on a daily basis, so it is easier for them to manage and ease the anxiety.

Be Kind Company. Monitoring your child's situation all the time is not going to give you any sort of positive result. Stay practical and positive rather than intense and controlling. This will get you nowhere—just locked out and avoided.

Lack of Inspiration or Stress and Anxiety. This could be the most important issue. Acknowledge that your youngster's laziness or irresponsibility could be a mask for his anxiety and self-disgust about his academics and schoolwork. (A lot more on this a bit later.)

Teach Life Equilibrium. As important as they are, life is not about school and work. Get involved with your child and help him become well rounded with extra-curricular tasks, relationships, and other functions outside of school.

Do Not Obsess over What the Future Holds. Don't place a critical spotlight on your kid all the time. Try to concentrate on his good characteristics and help him deal with the present.

Being on his or her case all the time is not going to give you any sort of favourable outcome. Stay kind and helpful instead of intense and controlling. This will certainly get you nowhere, just shut out and avoided.

Chapter 8:

HABITS

Advice on Compulsive Habits

It's normal for kids to become so concentrated on particular things that they seem almost obsessed with them. Maybe they like to arrange their playthings in a particular way or they twist or nibble their hair. Some routines are a natural, healthy, and balanced part of maturing. However, if they start to disrupt a child's life or cause them grief or damage, they can be classed as out of control.

Moms and dads will usually be able to tell the difference between something that's an organic part of growing up, and something that could require closer attention. For example, kids tend to be interested in scabs and will usually remove them to see if they bleed. That's different from chewing skin till it's sore just to produce a scab. In the same way, knuckle-cracking and nail-biting won't induce any harm unless done to extremes.

Hair-pulling appears benign enough . . . unless it's done so strongly that globs of hair are pulled out of the scalp. Children who regularly chew their hair may, in unusual situations, need surgery to get rid of hair balls. Some children's habits represent a comforting regimen, such as kissing all their preferred toys before bedtime. If these goodnight rituals begin to take longer and longer or have to be repeated over and over, it could a sign of a problem. Some kids become squeamish about dirt and germs from about four years of ages. While hand hygiene is a positive behaviour to encourage, washing the hands before or after touching anything or repeatedly washing them until the skin is raw, is not.

Why Do Habits Form?

Uncontrollable habits can appear at any age. They show a change in your youngster's life that confuses or frightens them and makes them want to gain back control. Examples include:

- Starting school
- Moving home
- A new sibling
- Bereavement
- Friendship problems
- Bullying
- Parents splitting up

A lot of grownups respond to stress in similar ways. Compulsive ideas and compulsions to do things are a normal response to stress and anxiety. Think about just how you feel simply before you take a vacation, as an example. If your head's full of things you need to remember, you might start to doubt whether you've secured the bathroom window or turned off the cooker. So you'll have the urge to return and inspect everything. It's typical for stressed-out kids to feel like that too.

Some kids might take care of stress and anxiety by regressing to earlier practices. If they stopped sucking their thumb, say, at two or three and the started again at six or seven, they might be trying to regain the sensation of protection they felt as infants.

As children age, uncontrollable behaviours are typically much more noticeable because they'll generally have left their babyhood behind.

Bad Habits/Annoying Behaviour

Bad Habits and Behaviours in Children

Parents find a lot of behaviours and habits of their youngsters irritating. It helps to first understand why your child is doing it when you wish to transform an undesirable behaviour. Often peccadillos are just a coping method. Your youngster could fall back on these behaviours when they are worried, bored, tired, annoyed, unhappy, insecure, or sleeping. Many of these "bad" routines are relaxing and calming to the child.

Many of these behaviours are just "stages" or routines, not serious health issues, and the child normally outgrows them. Handling them could be challenging. Generally, you need to get rid of bad habits. Yelling, calling attention to the behaviour, and punishment do not usually work to stop the habits (and may even increase it). Appreciation, good incentives, and patience are most likely to help.

Thumb and Finger Sucking and Pacifiers

There are different types of sucking little ones may do their infancy and childhood. Thumb and finger sucking typically begins in the first few months of life. Lots of children outgrow it well before their first birthday, and the majority do so by age five due to peer stress. Various other sucking objects include coverings and pacifiers. (Get some ideas on picking a safe pacifier from the American Academy of Paediatrics AAP.)

Sucking has a soothing, calming effect, and it commonly helps children have the ability to rest. It may become awkward when the permanent teeth start coming in (around age five) if the sucking alters the shape of the kid's teeth, bite, or palate. Get more information on this from the American Academy of Paediatric Dentistry. For even more pointers on the best ways to help your youngster stopped sucking, see the AAP's web page on how to help your youngster stop.

Head Banging, Head Rolling, and Body Rocking

Balanced movements consist of head banging, rolling, and body rocking. Head banging is when a kid consistently strikes his head against a solid object such as a crib, as much as eighty times in a row. This can be upsetting to moms and dads and health professionals worried about trauma. However, the youngster does not seem to be suffering, but rather calm and content. The practice often starts around the age of nine months and ceases by the age of two years. The episodes often last from fifteen times to a couple of hours, and they generally happen while the child is listening to songs or falling asleep.

When a baby rolls their head from side to side when lying on her spine, this is known as head rolling. They might also rub the hair completely off the back of their head.

Body rocking is when a kid rhythmically rocks while sitting or resting on their knees or elbows. This behaviour often starts around the age of six months and disappears by the age of two. Most kids rock for fifteen minutes or much less. Like head banging, it takes place while hearing songs or sleeping.

Head banging, head rolling, and body rocking are generally childhood self-comforting behaviours. These habits are usually benign, but they can be troubling if your child additionally has developmental delays. Talk about the behaviour with your paediatrician, who can help you determine whether there is any cause for alarm.

Teeth Grinding

Bruxism, or teeth clenching or grinding, is a practice seen in over half of all babies who develop regularly. It happens when the baby teeth come in and again around five years when the long-term teeth start to grow. It generally begins around the age of six months. Teeth grinding takes place mostly during sleep. The youngster generally outgrows it, although the bruxism might continue into their adult years. It can be worrying if it triggers dental issues or an ailment of the jaw joint and could require assessment by a dental professional.

Nail and Cuticle Biting or Picking

Your fingernails have a number of big tasks to do. They secure your fingertips and make it much easier for you to pick up very small items like loose strings. They likewise come in handy when you have an itch that really needs scratching.

When you bite your nails, your nails aren't there to do these things. And by biting them, you are breaking the skin and perhaps bringing bacteria into the openings in your skin. As a matter of fact, some individuals bite their cuticles and nails down until they bleed! When pathogens get into, they could get an infection.

Speaking of microorganisms, there are germs under their fingernails, so when they bite them, those pathogens can get into their mouth. Consider all the sickening stuff they touch all day long, like their sibling's drool-dripping pacifier, or stinky fitness centre socks, or slimy earthworms for their science work. You don't want those unpleasant bacteria getting inside their mouth.

If you wish them to quit biting their nails, it's a good decision! They might not realize they are doing it since nail attacking is a habit. Parents should ask, other members of the family, or friends to inform if they find your child biting their nails.

If discipline alone isn't really getting you anywhere, you may want to buy a special colourless nail gloss that makes their nails taste terrible. This could help your child to quit biting them. It could likewise help keep their nails trimmed and looking great.

Toenail attacking or cuticle biting and picking is an issue if it leads to infection of the nail or continual blood loss. As with various other habits, positive reinforcement approaches are the most efficient means to quit the behaviour. Try to catch your child without her finger in her mouth, and just describe what she is doing with her hands instead. "I see you are folding origami with your fingers" or "You are using your fingers to scratch the cat's ears! She likes it!"

Nose Picking

Nose picking is one of the most infuriating habits to moms and dads because it is among the least socially acceptable. However, it is one of the most common behaviours amongst adults and youngsters.

When crusting occurs from infection, allergic reactions, or small injuries, nose picking begins. Picking causes more irritation to the nose and could start a vicious circle. Picking is the most common cause of frequent nosebleeds.

Inform your youngster that picking is not acceptable in public, but that he can use a tissue to clean out the nose and take care of itching. If he picks his nose, explain that he is much more likely to get sick and pass his germs to others. Insist that he washes his hands after he picks or blows his nose. Often a little oil jelly a couple of times a day inside the nose will help to break the vicious circle of nose irritation and picking. Keeping the nose moist with a little saline aerosol can also help and is a better alternative for kids with asthma. Get in touch with your child's medical care supplier to discover what they suggest to reduce your youngster's nose inflammation.

Hair Twirling and Hair Pulling

Hair loss may be a sign of a medical problem such as infection or various other diseases. Your kid ought to see their doctor if they are losing hair.

On the other hand, hair twirling or mild hair pulling that results in a little hair loss is just another self-calming habit seen in babies and youngsters. Like thumb sucking, it usually takes place when the kid is loosened up, worn out, or tired. Children generally outgrow this behaviour by themselves.

There is a more severe kind of hair pulling, called trichotillomania, which entails pulling the hair from the scalp, eyelashes, eyebrows, or pubic areas. This is a rare ailment that typically suggests an underlying psychological problem and ought to be examined.

Because trichotillomania is a biological brain condition, it's not something that many individuals who have it can just stop doing when they feel like it. They typically need help from behaviour and healthcare professionals before they can quit. With the best help, however, most overcome their hair-pulling habit. Hair generally grows back when someone is able to stop pulling.

Getting rid of hair-pulling urges may include a particular sort of talk therapy called CBT (intellectual behaviour modification), medication, or a combination of both.

Specialists teach individuals with trichotillomania special strategies that help them to acknowledge the impulse to pull their hair before it becomes too strong to withstand. This can then help someone resist the urges so that they at some point grow weak and then go away.

To gather the information required to do this, a therapist will usually recommend keeping a diary of pulling episodes. A therapist can also assist people to regain confidence and feel better about themselves.

Because the urges and practices that lead to hair pulling are so ingrained, one can really feel much more tension or anxiety when first attempting to withstand the urge. That's why it helps to collaborate with a professional who can offer support and efficient assistance about how you can reverse these powerful influences.

After starting treatment, physicians can prescribe medicine if additional help is required. Some medicines can help the brain deal better with urges, making them much easier to withstand. Many individuals find it beneficial to keep their hands active with a different task (like pressing a stress ball, holding different items, or drawing) during activities or times when a pulling impulse is the strongest. Some people found that knitting while enjoying television helped keep their hands busy whenever they might really feel the urge to pull their hair.

On the other hand, hair twirling or light hair pulling that results in minimal hair loss is simply another self-calming habit seen in infants and youngsters. When somebody is able to quit pulling, hair often grows back.

Specialists teach people with trichotillomania special procedures that help them to recognize the impulse to pull hair before it becomes too strong to resist.

How to Break Your Child's Bad Habit

First, try to ignore the annoying behaviour. Your kid will probably outgrow the habit with time. Offering a lot of attention (even though it's negative) might actually encourage the behaviour.

Praise your child good habits. The best type of appreciation simply describes exactly what you see that you would like to see more of. For instance, tell them you saw they weren't chewing their nails.

It may be almost impossible to stop the problem until the youngster becomes interested in stopping. For example, a little girl could actually obtain enough "pleasure" from biting her nails that she will not be willing to quit. When she gets a little older, though, she might be interested in having good-looking nails. Then you will be able to help her quit.

If there are lots of behaviours you want to alter, start by focusing on a couple of the most dangerous or annoying ones. Do not try to make a lot of modifications all at once.

Try to find out just what may be making your youngster worried, and help him or her manage it. Give your kid opportunities to speak to you about things that could be causing stress. Make eye contact and actively pay attention.

Let your child make decisions whenever possible, by giving them acceptable choices. "Would you rather have toast or cereal for breakfast?" This will help your kid feel powerful, minimizing tension and frustration.

Redirect your kid and help them discover a better place or a better method to do what they are trying to do. If their nose is inflamed, have them clean it with a tissue, apply saline nasal apply or petrol jelly (consult your paediatrician for their referral), and then wash their hands. If they simply have to go "excavating", have them do it in the washroom, not in public, and wash their hands later.

Use natural or logical outcomes for troubling behaviour. The goal right here is to get children to make the right decision, not to bend them to your will. Be patient: it could take time for you to see results.

Be firm and kind. Follow up every time on sensible outcomes. Have a few positively mentioned rules, and explain the reasons behind them. Make certain your child understands the outcomes of breaking the policies.

Your child will possibly outgrow the bad habit with time. Giving them a lot of attention can actually encourage the behaviour.

The goal is to get little ones to make the best choice, not to bend them to your will.

How to Cope

If your youngsters have a compulsive routine, try to observe the trigger. Do they pull their hair when you leave them by themselves to watch television? Do they even realize they're doing it? Perhaps they're worried they're not getting enough attention? Try to retrain their brain by redirecting them to something different. Play a computer game with them or ask about what they're viewing instead.

- Remain calm rather than showing anger or irritation.
- Do not step in every time you see the uncontrollable behaviour; doing so may boost your kid's anxiety.
- Praise your child when he does something good, instead of criticizing the habit.
- Give your kid the chance to tell you just how she's feeling. She might understand that talking about the habit is a much better way to take care of anxiety.
- Sit down as a family once a week to talk about how things are for everyone.

Every Child Is Different

Do not assume there's a problem if your child has compulsive behaviours that none of his friends have. It has to do with you as a parent knowing your child, rather than "one size fits all." A much better clue to just what's taking place is whether your child is troubled about the situation and how satisfied they appear to be in general. If you're in doubt, it's best to see your GP.

Do not leave this chapter too quickly. Practice the exercises given, with the assurance that the results will take you as far as you wish. It is important to understand this chapter before going to the next one.

Chapter 9:

TEACHING KIDS ABOUT MONEY

Teaching children self-discipline with money is one of the most important life skills that you can teach your child. Regrettably, many little ones grow up without understanding the best ways to budget, pay expenses, or save money. This can cause young adults to get deeply into debt and make inadequate financial choices.

Instructing children about money takes discipline. It requires making them earn their own money and helping them spend it intelligently. It also involves speaking to them about the best ways to make important financial decisions. Children are never too young to begin knowing about saving and spending money.

Allow Them to Earn Money

One of the very best ways to help children start understanding money is to let them make their own. Just as most adults go to work to earn their money, kids have to discover the best ways to work to earn their cash.

Give your little ones age-appropriate tasks. Designate daily and weekly tasks that allow your child to make money. Additionally, offer opportunities to make even more money if your child plans to work a lot more.

If he does not earn it, it's important not to give your child the money. I've worked with plenty of moms and dads who say their kids simply aren't inspired to earn money. Nonetheless, it's normally because the little ones get every little thing they want all the time, so there is no need for their very own money!

Decide just what you buy for your kid and what you will not. For instance, if your kid wants a brand-new computer game, don't just rush out to buy it. As an alternative, enable your kid to acquire it with his own hard-earned money and he'll cherish it a lot much more.

Or if you have a young adult who wants to go to the movies on Friday night, do not simply turn over the money right away. As an alternative, make your young adult pay for extras like this. This helps adolescents learn how much things cost and can help them start making decisions about what they want to accomplish with their hard-earned money.

Develop a Budgeting Plan

Work with kids to develop a kid-friendly spending plan. Most little ones need help knowing the amount of money to save and how much to spend.

An excellent way to help kids learn about money is to show them that a specific portion of their cash has to be saved. Think about ten, twenty, or thirty per cent of their allowance to be saved each week. For kids, separate piggy banks can be a great way to help them break down their cash into saving and spending.

For older youngsters, help them open up a bank account. Then, they can start learning about how to transfer and take out money. This can also teach them the best ways to gain interest, and you can begin having conversations about investing.

Identify exactly what values you intend to teach your children. For some parents, it is very important to teach kids how to give to charity. Think about motivating your kid to set aside a particular amount of money that will be given away to church, a charity, or used to purchase presents for others.

Setting Goals

It is essential to teach children ways to set targets for their money. Saving for an automobile or for a college fund are reasonable objectives for teenagers. Help younger kids save up for a special event or a toy of their choosing.

It can be practical to show little ones just how long it takes to achieve objectives. If your youngster earns $10 a week, review how long it will take to get that brand new skateboard. Help kids make good choices about how much to spend on their purchases, and review how different selections might offer different prices and quality.

Provide Consequences When Necessary

Supply positive and negative outcomes for your child's money management. As an example, provide bunches of appreciation and positive reinforcement when children are working doggedly to stick to a spending plan. Don't allow their effort to go unnoticed.

Make sure there are unfavourable repercussions for blunders. Often it makes sense to allow children to experience natural repercussions. For instance, if a youngster takes $30 with him to the fair and he spends everything within the first couple of minutes, don't offer him more money. Rather, the outcome is that he won't be able to have a good time after spending all his money.

At other times, it makes sense to take away privileges. If you have a child that argues, lies, or steals, there needs to be a much more severe outcome. For example, do not let him go places with friends or take away his electronics.

Useful Tips on Teaching Kids about Money

It's never ever premature to begin training children about money. Grade-school age is a perfect time for teaching kids about money, given that they are being taught addition, subtraction, and other math principles at school. Parents can establish some important fiscal skills, such as saving, even with younger grade-schoolers. As kids get older, they can begin to make some choices about money, such as deciding how they can spend their allowance or even helping you choose ways to designate cash for things to do while on vacation. Below are ten great tips on training little ones about money.

- Play computer games that involve teaching kids about money. Parlour games such as Monopoly and Life can be a fun way for little ones to find out about money. Gather your entire family around your favourite game and allow your grade-schooler to unleash her internal business magnate.
- Take your kid shopping. Educating kids about money can be a part of everyday family routines, such as visiting the supermarket. Inform your child just what your spending plan is and make a game of purchasing exactly what you require under that set quantity. Clip discount coupons, and let your grade-schooler help you discover products on sale. A nine- or ten-year-old can take a calculator and help you make note of your purchases—and figure the amount you've saved.
- Give him an allowance. By grade school, kids are able to do even more chores to help around your house. Whether or not you connect duties to an allowance, it's a great concept to get your grade-schooler into the routine of managing her own cash.
- Encourage her to save. You can use an adorable piggy bank you choose together or a favourite Hello Kitty pocketbook. Whatever it is, decide on a place where she can keep her money. Some specialists recommend giving your youngster three different receptacles to place her cash—one for saving, one for spending, and one for giving away to charity. You could determine together exactly how to break down her weekly allowance among the three containers.

- Take it to the bank. Take your child to the financial institution and open up an account. When he leaves it in the bank, explain to him that his cash will grow.
- Teach the best ways to talk about money. My seven-year-old once asked someone we know exactly how much money she made. It was an innocent mistake. Grade-schoolers are often wondering about everything—how much somebody's home cost or what somebody earns. They normally have no concept of what that number might mean; one of my boy's friends once stated that his parents paid $500 for their house! Delicately explain to your child that it's not respectful to ask people how much money they spend or make.
- Curb television time. Little ones can see an incredible number of commercials in a really short period of time. Grownups have trouble battling the impact, so just how can you expect a ten-year-old (let alone a five-year-old) to be unsusceptible to the appeal of the most recent toy or gadget?
- Discuss credit cards and ATM cards. Younger grade-schoolers might believe that money just appears out of ATM machines or that you can simply pay for everything with a credit card. Even older grade-schoolers might not totally comprehend exactly what it means to use credit (that paying for everything with a card usually means paying interest).
- Set an example. And always place spending into context, emphasizing that things alone do not make people happy. Remind your children that there are far more important things, like spending time together, that don't set you back a penny.
- Show kindness. No course about money is complete without some conversation concerning charity. Help her put money in context by showing her that there are lots of other things, such as love of family and our fellow man, that are important.

Chapter 10:

REWARD SYSTEMS

Reward systems provide a great positive discipline method to help children discover how to take responsibility for handling their own behaviour. Reward systems teach kids to earn their privileges. Along with various other self-control techniques, reward systems can be a great addition to a detailed behaviour management strategy. When they are used as component of an age-appropriate self-control strategy, kids from young children to teens can benefit from earning rewards.

Reward Systems for Toddlers and Pre-Schoolers

Toddlers and pre-schoolers can usually take advantage of straightforward sticker label charts. Allow little ones to decorate their plans to get them inspired to gain stickers. Then choose sticker labels that your youngster will be happy about making.

Make sure the sticker label graph is presented plainly in your house. Young children are typically extremely pleased about their accomplishments and want to ensure that everyone knows they have made sticker labels. Use appreciation to help keep them inspired to go on making stickers.

Select one habit to work with each time. Habits that could function well with a sticker label plan. Supply a sticker promptly after you see the preferred habits, as this will give a positive consequence that will increase their motivation to do it once again.

Reward Systems for School-Age Children

School-age children can manage a somewhat intricate reward system. Sticker labels alone are not typically a sufficient incentive at all. As an alternative, they can benefit from trading sticker labels for larger rewards.

For example, a seven-year-old can profit from knowing that when she makes three sticker labels she can go to the playground. Youngsters of this age are able to put off gratification a little, but not for too long. So ensure they can win rewards regularly. Depending upon your child, a reward might be needed daily, every few days, or weekly.

Clarify the reward system to your child. Inform her, "When you make three sticker labels, we will go to the park to play. This is how you gain sticker labels . . ." Give your kid the opportunity to ask questions and suggest benefits she will be able to earn.

Reward Systems for Tweens

Tweens can take advantage of a lot more challenging systems with bigger incentives. Keep in mind that incentives do not need to cost you money.

Also, rewards do not need to be additional things your child makes. As an alternative, you could make use of privileges that your youngster already has. Rather than eliminating privileges for misbehaviours, allow your child to earn privileges, such as watching television or using the computer system, online video, or telephone computer games. Make these privileges that must be earned.

Tweens may feel too old for "stickers", so you could develop a system where they earn check marks or tokens. A token economic climate system allows them to earn tokens throughout the day that can be exchanged for privileges. For example, two tokens could be equivalent to half an hour of television.

Pick up to three behaviours to resolve at a time. Choose the one habit that your youngster currently does fairly well. This could help your kid feel happy, which is very important in keeping tweens motivated.

Reward Systems for Teenagers

Young adults will certainly grow out of professional reward charts and systems. Nonetheless, this does not mean you need to do away with reward systems completely. It is very important to continue to connect privileges to good behaviour.

For example, make the privilege of spending time with friends on the weekends dependent on a teen getting all of his homework done punctually for the week. Only permit a teen to borrow the vehicle if he has actually done every one of his chores promptly throughout the week. Do not give teens money unless they have earned it.

Electronics are an additional opportunity that works well for a lot of teens. Consider allowing them their cell-phone privileges every day right after their homework and chores are finished. Just make sure that you develop clear guidelines beforehand to ensure that they know just what is expected of them each day.

Chapter 11:

PUNISHMENT AND DISCIPLINE

When it comes to parenting youngsters, there's a big difference between punishment and discipline. When children make errors, they depend on adult treatment to help guide and show them their mistakes. Nonetheless, the numerous techniques moms and dads need to intervene can make a big difference in a kid's ability to recover from mistakes.

What Is Punishment?

Punishment is an intervention that applies a penalty for a child's offense. It often arises from a parent's sensations of irritation and desperation. It usually offers kids the message "I misbehaved." Commonly the focus is on the parent attempting frantically to keep control and trying to show to the youngster "I'm in charge whether you like it or not."

Authoritarian moms and dads frequently provide penalties to youngsters. When kids ask why they cannot do something, they are frequently told, "Because I said so." These sorts of answers usually give kids the message that their opinions don't matter and that they do not have the capacity to make any kind of choices for themselves.

An example of a punishment would be something such as paddling. If a youngster strikes his brother and then gets a paddling from his parent, he learns, "I'm bad. Mom hits me." Other examples of punishment include things such as a young adult getting grounded for ever or when a mom and dad throw away a youngster's toys.

The Problems with Punishments

There are numerous problems with punishments. One issue is that kids are not shown the best ways to act. If a youngster hits his brother and after that gets a spanking, he is not shown what to do the next time he feels upset with his sibling.

Punishment likewise teaches children that they are not able to be in control of themselves. They usually discover that their moms and dads must manage their habits and feelings because they are not able to do so alone. They also tend to not have the capacity to make good choices since their moms and dads have always made their choices for them.

When kids get regular punishments, they most likely grow up to be assertive and unfavourable. When they get punished, they usually concentrate on how angry they feel towards their moms and dads instead of considering how they can recover from their error. Moms and dads who give punishments also tend to be inconsistent much of the time, which can provoke anxiety in little ones.

Parents may choose to use physical punishment (such as spanking) to stop undesirable behaviour. The largest drawback to this method is that although the punishment stops the bad behaviour for some time, it doesn't get your kid to change his or her habits. Disciplining your child is actually simply instructing him or her to select good behaviours. If your child does not know a good behaviour, they are most likely to return to the bad behaviour. Physical punishment becomes much less efficient with time and can cause the youngster to behave strongly. It could likewise be held to be border on child abuse. Various other methods of punishment are better and should be used whenever feasible.

What Is Discipline?

Self-control concentrates on teaching kids new capabilities, such as ways to manage their behaviours, deal with issues, and handle their feelings. Discipline focuses on training little ones to recover from their errors and find better ways to resolve problems in the future.

Self-control strategies include things such as the time-out. For example, if a child blows up and tosses a toy, he is given a time-out where he can relax. The objective of a time-out is to show youngsters how you can calm them down when they are disturbed and to ensure that in the future they can find time-out by themselves before they throw a toy.

Discipline takes a definitive technique and allows kids to discover options based on their behaviour. When they are given adverse outcomes, the repercussions make good sense and are time-sensitive. As an example, a child that does not eat all of his dinner is not allowed to have dessert, but he is told he can have dessert the next evening if wants it.

Self-control includes some proactive methods to promote new capabilities, such as by making using of praise or reward systems. Discipline also helps foster a positive relationship between kids and parents; children who are often given positive attention will reduce their attention-seeking habits.

There are a lot of efficient self-control approaches that parents can make use of to teach children how to become responsible adults. Age-appropriate discipline techniques help little ones really feel protected in their partnerships with others and promotes healthy and balanced self-confidence. Discipline is a caring way to show little ones your wish to keep them safe, teach them to make healthy choices for themselves, and gain freedom.

The Biggest Discipline Mistakes Parents Make

Use discipline with your child in a way that will be most efficient in teaching him everything he needs to know before he turns eighteen. This can appear like an impossible job. Here are some of the biggest discipline mistakes a lot of parents make; find out what you can do about them.

Not Offering the Right Type of Attention

When children don't get enough good attention, behaviour problems frequently result. Positive attention reduces attention-seeking behaviours such as whining, tantrums, and other purposely annoying behaviours. When kids do not get attention for good behaviours, such as playing quietly, sitting at the table, and taking turns, they'll typically act up simply to obtain any sort of attention.

Spending fifteen minutes each day giving your kid your undistracted attention can reduce a lot of negative habits and can help create a positive connection. Praise is another terrific way to offer kids good attention. Many more professional ways to offer positive attention feature things such as reward programs or token economic climate systems.

Only Checking Out the Short-Term

One big parenting mistake is to concentrate only on the short-term. Great discipline strategies must additionally concentrate on the long-lasting. It is necessary to keep in mind that your child will need certain capabilities in order to become a healthy, accountable grownup. The most effective discipline methods focus on teaching little ones these capabilities.

As an example, in an effort to make today's trip to the store more tolerable, some moms and dads give in to little ones when their children are whining. Giving in teaches children that whining and grumbling is a good way to get their needs satisfied. Consequently, it is important to know just how this is likely to affect a youngster in various other situations in his life. A youngster who finds out that grumbling gets his demands satisfied will not have a lot of friends, as his peers will certainly become irritated by him.

Youngsters need to learn that there are unfavourable outcomes for their habits. When moms and dads stick to restrictions and provide fair, consistent, factual discipline methods, youngsters will discover the skills they require.

Absence of Clear and Consistent Rules

It can be quite perplexing to kids to understand exactly what is expected from them when there are not clear policies. Often the trouble is that each mom and dad has a different rule or interpretation of the rule. This results in youngsters viewing one parent as the "hero" and the other parent as the "villain".

At other times, the trouble is that a parent is not consistent. Stress from various other duties such as a job, can make a parent feel too tired to follow up with restrictions and repercussions. An overworked single mother might feel too tired to make her kid do his homework some evenings. This can be confusing to him and may cause him to say a lot more on the nights she tries to get him to finish his homework, making her feel it just isn't worth the trouble.

Establishing family regulations helps youngsters have more structure. When children are certain just what the outcomes and limits are, they can make more knowledgeable decisions. It is very important that children also have assigned chores and clear rules about money to teach them responsibility.

Not Having a Discipline Plan.

When it comes to taking care of behaviour concerns, it is better to be proactive rather than responsive. Take a while to create a comprehensive habits strategy to help take care of behaviour concerns. When moms and dads attack issues with a clear strategy, it is a lot easier to track the child's progress and make changes when needed.

Without a clear plan, parents sometimes struggle to take care of behaviours, and the result is turmoil. As an example, if a kid starts striking others, a parent might not know how to manage the child's hostility. The parent might sometimes use break but at other times might spank the youngster out of exasperation. This incongruity might be puzzling to the child and might not stop the behaviour.

Parents need to create a behaviour administration strategy whenever behaviour problems come up with their youngsters. This will improve consistency and guarantee that children are getting clear messages about their behaviours. It will likewise help moms and dads to cooperate with other caretakers to make certain that all the grownups are responding in a comparable manner.

Discovering how to discipline your child in a way that will be most effective in teaching him everything he needs to learn before he turns eighteen can seem like an impossible task. When moms and dads attack problems with a clear plan, it is much simpler to track the kid's improvement and make changes when necessary.

Parenting Mistakes

- Do you get tired of hearing yourself lecture your child? If yes, chances are you are speaking too much and not listening closely enough.
- Not growing along with your youngster. When the child is ten, moms and dads can't make use of the same techniques as they did when their child was five.
- Focusing on unfavourable behaviours and paying attention to your child only when they do something you do not approve of. You grow exactly what you praise. That is what you will certainly see if you concentrate on the bad habits.
- Informing children what they shouldn't do instead of what they must do. Offer your youngster examples of habits that you wish them to copy.
- Responding to kids just after they have made a mistake. Moms and dads should establish rules for their youngsters

before problems occur, not in feedback about troubles that have actually developed.
- Forgetting to have a good time with each other.

Types of Parenting Styles

The sort of self-control you use can have a remarkable impact on your child's advancement. Your discipline approaches have a large effect on the type of partnership you have with your kid. Your self-control techniques can also affect a kid's state of mind and temperament into adulthood.

Analysts have actually found four sorts of parenting styles. These various styles hinge on what the parents really feel the kid needs from them. Therefore, each parenting style uses a different method of discipline.

Authoritarian Parenting

Authoritarian parenting is where parents set up the regulations and expect that kids will follow them without exception. Kids have little to no involvement in analysing difficulties or challenges. Instead, parents expect that children will follow every one of the guidelines all the time.

If youngsters test the guidelines or ask why, they are usually told, "Because I said so." Kids are not normally given the reasons for the rules, and there is little room for any negotiation. Authoritarian parents may use punishments instead of rewards.

Kids who grow up with authoritarian parents tend to adhere to rules a lot of the time; they can develop problems with self-confidence. Sometimes youngsters become aggressive as they focus a lot more on being angry at their parents for the punishment instead of knowing the best ways to solve problems and make choices.

Definitive Parenting

Definitive parents also have policies that children are expected to follow, but they allow some exceptions to the rules. They usually tell youngsters the reasons for the policies, and they are more likely to think about a child's feelings when establishing limitations.

Definitive parents tend to use outcomes as opposed to punishments. They also use more positive consequences to reinforce good behaviours and may be a lot more willing compared to authoritarian moms and dads to use reward systems and praise.

Children who grow up with authoritative discipline tend to be satisfied and successful. They are often good at assessing and making choices on their own. They frequently grow up to be responsible adults who really feel comfortable revealing their opinions.

Permissive Parenting

Permissive parents do not provide much discipline to their youngsters. They tend to be lenient and may just step in when there is a severe problem. There might be some consequences for misbehaviours, but they commonly have the attitude that "kids will be kids."

Permissive parents may take on more of the role of a good friend than a parent. They might encourage their kids to talk with them about their problems, but they may not inhibit a lot of bad habits.

Children who grow up with permissive moms and dads tend to have a hard time academically. They might exhibit more behavioural troubles, as they will likely not appreciate authority and policies. They usually have reduced self-confidence and could suffer a great deal of unhappiness.

Uninvolved Parenting

Uninvolved parents tend to be neglectful. They frequently do not satisfy their children's fundamental needs and might expect children to grow up by themselves. Occasionally this is due to a parent's psychological problems or drug abuse issues. They may likewise lack knowledge about parenting and childhood development, or they might really feel overwhelmed by life's other problems.

Uninvolved moms and dads tend to have little knowledge of what their youngsters are doing. There often few if any assumptions or guidelines. Children may not receive any nurturing or advice, and they lack the necessary parental attention.

Children usually tend to lack self-esteem, and they do poorly academically when moms and dads are uninvolved. They also show regular behaviour troubles and rank low in happiness.

Determining a Discipline Strategy

Sometimes parents do not fit just one category. There might be times when they are more authoritarian and times when they often be more definitive, and their discipline methods might vary from child to child.

When figuring out a discipline method, it is very important to think about what it is that you want your child to know. Efficient discipline approaches can teach children to become responsible adults who are able to make healthy choices on their own.

Positive Discipline Techniques

Positive discipline is among the five primary types of self-control that can take care of a variety of behaviour problems. Nonetheless, many parents question whether good self-control truly works. Before leaping to any verdicts, it is very important to learn about a few of the essential principles of positive discipline.

Develop a Positive Partnership

Proponents of positive discipline advise that caregivers spend quality time with children every single day to build a healthy and balanced relationship. This quality time could consist of having fun, chatting, or simply enjoying one another's company.

During this quality time, it can be beneficial to talk to your kid about the feelings he experienced throughout the day. Ask him when he felt the saddest and when he felt the happiest. Then, share the very same things about your day. This supplies a chance to learn about each other and build a strong basis for the connection, while also teaching about feelings.

Use Encouragement Liberally

Positive discipline concentrates on encouragement. Instead of praising kids for a job well done, reassurance focuses on a youngster's efforts, even if there isn't really an effective outcome. Encouragement needs to celebrate a child's improvement while motivating him to keep trying.

Encouragement can help kids identify their full potential. It also shows them to be a lot more independent, as they will begin to see just what they are capable of doing on their own. The trick is to encourage children in a manner that makes them feel appreciated and recognized, as good discipline is based on the belief that all children need to really feel a deep sense of belonging.

Designing how you can take care of blunders is a vital part of favourable self-control. For example, when you slip up with parenting, acknowledge it and say sorry to your youngster. This shows kids the importance of taking responsibility for their own behaviours and shows the value of learning from errors.

Problem Solve Together

Caretakers are urged to meet problem-solving concerns as they develop. This teaches kids important analytical skills while offering them opportunities to share their views. Mutual respect is a fundamental part of the procedure.

Positive discipline highlights the importance of kids having tasks. Little ones provide input about exactly what tasks they intend to complete. This potential to have input in to their tasks provides them with a greater sense of belonging and encourages them to complete their tasks.

Training is an essential step in the process. Youngsters are offered clear guidelines regarding what is expected of them. Moms and dads take time to teach youngsters how to clean their room or the best way to do their washing. This provides children with a chance to ask questions and can remove misconceptions about their tasks.

Positive discipline makes use of an authoritarian approach, where a youngster's feelings are considered. Kids are motivated to share about their feelings and also review their errors, concepts, and issues openly. Parents then collaborate with the child on resolving problems working together in respectful interaction.

Use Discipline Instead Punishments

Positive discipline makes a sharp distinction between discipline and punishment. Consequences are not meant to be punitive, but instead they need to supply long-term consequences that teach life lessons that prepare youngsters to become responsible grownups.

Time-out is not considered a punishment. Instead, it needs to be referred to as a positive time out and needs to occur in an enjoyable, comfortable location. A pleasant break is designed to teach children to take a time-out when they need to cool down so that they can at some point take a break by themselves without being made to.

When to Use Positive Discipline

Positive discipline works well with pre-school kids and with teenagers. Many schools are motivating teachers to make use of positive discipline in the classroom by employing the exact same principles. Positive discipline is likely to be efficient for any type of caregiver and can help guarantee that youngsters are learning from their mistakes.

Self-Discipline

The primary objective should be for parents to work themselves out of a job. At some point, your kids shouldn't require you at all. In order to help them with this, moms and dads need to help little ones learn self-discipline.

Children need to learn self-discipline in relation to money, chores, homework, and time management. In order to teach self-discipline, there should be consistent repercussions for misbehaviour. There should also be positive consequences, such as reward systems or praise, for acting sensibly.

When parents do things like forcing children to do their homework, it doesn't teach self-discipline. Rather, the mom and dad end up taking more responsibility for getting the task done than the kid. Ordering, pleading with, and asking children to do something commonly makes a kid focus on his anger toward his mom and dad rather than taking responsibility.

Helping Children Develop Self-Discipline

Among the primary tasks of very early childhood is to develop self-discipline. Parents frequently find themselves correcting their kids for disrupting, being wild, not following directions, or for not controlling their mouths or hands. These situations all require self-control or self-discipline. Children are by nature impulsive. Some children actually have different organic elements that increase impulsiveness. Part of the solution for impulse control is to discover self-control. A youngster equipped with self-control has an incredible asset for taking care of life's challenges. Numerous relational and personal problems can be avoided or controlled when one has self-control. Below are some ideas for teaching it to children.

- Teach children to come when they are called. When parents call a child, that child shouldn't yell, "What?" from a different room, from across the parking lot, or from the far side of the playing field. Children should learn to come within a few feet of the parent in order to have a conversation with the parent. This helps children learn that self-control often suggests that we should give up what we are doping in order to do something else.
- Show children to react positively to correction. Most youngsters do not like to be disciplined and react badly in either active (temper) or passive (attitude) ways. This is undesirable and ends up being a great opportunity to teach self-control. Among the facts of life is that individuals commonly must follow directions which might not be their inclination. Teach children to respond with a good attitude as well as with the correct behaviour. This requires self-control and helps children learn to regulate their impulses. A good response to correction is sometimes tough to learn, but work in this area will help children establish a skill which will help them for life.
- Many social skills call for self-control. When they demonstrate this top quality and factor try to appreciate your youngster. Listening closely, knowing when and how to disturb, controlling anger, and reporting back after finishing a task all call for self-discipline.
- Motivate children to tackle tasks which teach discipline. These might include sporting activities, song courses, a paper route, caring for a next-door neighbour's pet,

memorizing scripture, keeping a tidy room, or a host of other tasks.

- When a child receives a reward such as payment for a job completed or even a star on a chart or a special treat, discuss self-discipline. External incentives provide a great opportunity to talk about interior incentives. The actual benefit of a paper route is not the money but the building of self-control. "You are quite mature and responsible to get up every morning." "I know you would rather have conformed, but I like the way you required time to walk the puppy. That shows self-discipline."

- Use bedtime to teach self-discipline. Some youngsters have a difficult time going to sleep without starting a fight, and this becomes a great opportunity to teach self-discipline to kids. It requires a whole lot of self-control for a kid to stay quietly in bed while mom and dad are still awake. Set a bedtime, create a routine that includes all the necessary bedtime tasks, and work at getting your kid to stay in bed without a parent sleeping in the room. This needs work on the part of the parent, but it will certainly pay significant dividends in the long run.

- Morning programs, duties, and household routines become opportunities for youngsters to discover responsibility and self-control. Being responsible is "doing the proper thing even when nobody is watching". The rewards for being responsible are called privileges. The kid who is able to get everything sorted out and be at breakfast by 7:30 a.m. is allowed the privilege of staying up past their 8:00 p.m. bedtime. Being allowed to decide on one's clothes is the reward for getting dressed before the deadline. Simple perks of life are seen as privileges connected with responsibility.

Some moms and dads attempt to offer their children a simpler life than they had, or they attempt to make their children feel good at the expense of good character. Actually, spoiled youngsters are not happy, while self-disciplined kids frequently are!

Before beginning the next chapter, pause a moment for contemplation. Review mentally what you have read in this one. If the contents do not clearly come back to you, read it again.

It would be impossible to place a cash value on what you have just learned. Do not allow yourself to forget a bit of it.

Chapter 12:

HELPING CHILDREN DEAL WITH THEIR ANGER

Temper is like the mercury in a thermometer. When left uncontrolled, the intensity of the emotional state rises from irritation to anger and then to other points like rage and resentment. As its magnitude grows, people close themselves off from relationships. Having a plan to handle anger can restrict its strength and prevent much of the devastation temper tends to trigger.

Controlling Anger and Resentment

Most families don't prepare for temper. They somehow simply go on, hoping things will improve. Lots of family members don't fix their anger but simply keep trying to start over. Starting over may be valuable sometimes, but it has a tendency to neglect the trouble instead of resolve it. Here are some concepts for managing temper in your family.

Anger is good for identifying problems but not good for solving them. One of the problems individuals encounter is the shame they feel after they've gotten angry. There are lots of additional complexes and the circumstance which can arose the anger. God made us as psychological beings, and emotions are valuable for offering us clues about our environment. Anger, specifically, points out problems. It uncovers things that are wrong. Some of those things are inside us and call for modifications to our expectations or demands. Other issues are external and need to be taken care of in a useful way. Helping children understand that temper is useful for identifying problems but bad for resolving them is the first step toward a healthy and balanced anger management strategy.

Recognize the early warning signs of anger. Children frequently don't acknowledge anger. Actually, times they act up before they recognize what has happened. Recognizing the early signs helps kids become a lot more knowledgeable about their feelings, which in turn offers them a much better chance to control their responses to these feelings. Exactly how can you tell when you're getting upset? How can your children recognize aggravation before it gets out of control?

Here are some typical cues in youngsters which suggest that they are becoming angry and may blow up.

- Tensed up physical body
- Clenched teeth
- Greater intensity of speech or behaviour
- Angry words or the tone of voice changing to whining or yelling
- Restlessness, withdrawal, unresponsiveness, or being conveniently prompted
- Noises with the mouth like growls or deep breathing
- Sulking
- Squinting, rolling the eyes, or other facial expressions

Find out how to recognize the signs that your youngster is starting to get frustrated. Try to find indicators that come prior to the eruption. When you understand the signs, start to point them out to your kid. Make observations and teach your child to acknowledge those signs. Ultimately children will be able to see their very own frustration and anger and choose appropriate responses before it's too late. They'll be able to move from the feeling to the appropriate actions, but initially they need to be able to acknowledge the cues that anger is growing.

Step back. Teach your youngster to step back from the difficult situation and to withdraw for a few minutes. One of the healthiest responses to anger at any one of its phases is to step back. Then the youngster can reconsider the circumstances, calm down, and decide what to do next. Frustrations can quickly build, rage can be devastating, and anger is always damaging to the one who is angry. Stepping back can help the child stop the progress of anger and figure out how to respond in different ways.

The length of the break is determined by the strength of the emotional state. A kid that is merely irritated could simply take a deep breath. A youngster who is completely enraged most likely needs to walk out and leave the room.

Choose a better response. After the child has stepped back and settled down, then it's time to pick a better response to the situation. What should they do? Moms and dads who attend to anger in their youngsters frequently react harmfully, mentioning the wrong without suggesting options.

There are three positive choices: talk about it, obtain help, or reduce and persevere. Streamlining the choices makes the choice procedure simpler. When they know there are three choices, even young children can learn to react constructively to disappointment. These choices are really opportunities to be discovered. Youngsters commonly abuse them or excessively depend on just one. Take some time to teach your youngsters these skills and practice them as responses to angry feelings.

Never ever attempt to reason with a child who is enraged. In some cases kids become enraged. The main way to tell when children are enraged is that they can no longer think reasonably and their anger is now controlling them. Several parents try to talk their kids out of temper, commonly leading to even more intensity. The child that is enraged has actually lost control. You may see clenched fists, squinting eyes, or a host of venting behaviours. Anger is just one of those feelings that can grab you before you know what's happening. The magnitude can grow from aggravation to anger to eruption before anybody realizes it.

Whether it's the two-year-old having a tantrum or the fourteen-year-old ranting and raving, do not get drawn into dialogue. It only increases the problem. Discussing it is important, however. Hang around till after the child has settled down.

When emotions leave control, take a break from the dialogue. Sometimes children and moms and dads are having a discussion about something and moods flare. Mean words usually push buttons which inspire additional mean words and anger escalates. Stop the procedure, take a break and resume the dialogue after people have actually settled.

Be proactive in training kids about anger management, controlling frustration, and reducing rage. Model, discuss, review, and teach your kids about temper. Talk about examples of aggravation and temper seen in children's video clips.

When temper issues seem out of hand or you simply have no idea exactly what to do, obtain help. Occasionally a third party can offer valuable suggestions and rules to inspire your family to manage anger in a more useful way. Children can begin to develop bitterness and resentment in their lives and may need assistance to manage it. Unresolved anger can create issues in relationships later on. Kids do not outgrow resentment, they turn into it. Professional assistance might be required.

Helping Kids Learn Self-Control

By discovering self-control, children can make good choices and react to difficult circumstances in ways that can yield positive outcomes.

For instance, if you state that you're not serving ice cream until after supper, your youngster may cry, plead, or even scream in the hope that you will give in. With self-control, your kid can recognize that a mood outburst indicates you'll take away the ice cream for good and that it's smarter to wait with patience.

Tips on Teaching Your Teen How to Deal with Stress

Take some time out of your week for some individualized time with your child. Make this a regular component of your routine so that he will know that he can count on you being there.

Encourage healthy escapes from the daily grind of their school. Tell your teen about the benefits of taking the dog out for a run, hiking a trail, or simply going out for a stroll. Exercising is known to alleviate anxiety. Creativity will also help to relieve tension. Buy your young adult a diary or daily record or encourage another innovative leisure activity.

Laughter can remove anxiety just as much as physical exercise and is another healthy and balanced retreat. Make amusing or funny publications readily available in your house. Allow get-togethers with friends. Rent motion pictures with a comedy motif. You could also show your teen ways to laugh at himself, using humour to take the tension out of typical human errors that can happen to anyone.

Build your young ones self-confidence by remembering to praise him when he does something good. With the basic structure of assurance and confidence that you give, your young adult will certainly be much better able to handle modifications and anxiety.

Teach your teenager ways to keep things in perspective. This is a fundamental part of relieving anxiety. Taking a situation and looking at it from different angles and seeing how it connects in the whole scheme of life are skills your teen will need to discover. He will be able to reduce his tension load if he has the ability to let go of the little stress triggers we run into in our lives.

Show your teenager ways to concentrate on the good aspects of a situation. Have him try to list the opportunities created rather than the problems posed. Even the most unpleasant experiences could result in positive growth and results.

Watch out for negative roadblocks. Commonly, teens who do not find out the best ways to handle anxiety properly depend on alcohol and drugs. Speak to your teen often about these obstructions, and bear in mind the warning signs. Show your young adult the advantages of taking the dog out for a jog or just going out for a walk.

Develop your teen's confidence and self-worth by remembering to praise him when he does something great. With the basic structure of assurance and confidence that you give, your teen will certainly be much better able to deal with changes and tension.

Taking a situation, looking at it from different perspectives, and seeing how it fits in to the entire pattern of life is a skill your teenager will really need to discover. Often, young adults who do not find out how to deal with anxiety appropriately turn to drugs and alcohol.

Chapter 13:

SOCIAL SKILLS

Children really need help honing and exercising brand new social skills. Young kids have to know how to use their words so they don't become aggressive and to ensure they can establish healthy and balanced relationships.

Train younger children in standard social skills, such as making eye contact and taking turns in a conversation. Establish session where children can practice making use of social skills. Supply them with responses and praise.

Older children often need some high quality adjusting with their social skills. Role play how you can ask for help, speak up when their feelings are hurt, or resist a bully. Having appropriate social skills can make a big difference in a child's progress through their school and into adulthood.

How to Develop Social Skills in Children

Creating social skills in youngsters prepares them for a lifetime of healthier communications in all facets of life. Social skills are an essential component of functioning in society. Showing good manners, connecting properly with others, being considerate of the feelings of others, and expressing individual needs are all essential parts of strong social skills. Helping kids to acquire these important skills demands a different set of techniques in each stage of development.

Infants

Demonstrate social skills to babies. Infants appreciate social interaction as shown by their smiles and coos. At this phase, infants are only familiar with their own necessities and desires.

- Talk to babies. When they sob and make noises, react to them in your normal language. This motivates infants to attempt to talk to you.
- Train them to think about others. By replying to their needs and cries, you are teaching babies to be considerate of the requirements of others.
- Provide attention and love. Kissing and holding infants is important for their social development. It's a fundamental necessity at this stage and ought to not be confused with spoiling a child with too much attention.
- Be calm around infants. A crying child who has actually kept you up all night might leave you feeling irritated. Nonetheless, taking deep breaths and calming yourself prior to holding an infant will model a harmonious social atmosphere.

Toddlers and Pre-Schoolers

Teach young children to respect people and their property. In the toddler stage, kids have access to some words and basic sentences. They tend to play alone and aren't yet good about sharing toys or various other items.

- Create a social atmosphere in the home. Invite other moms and dads and kids over to expose kids to different individuals.
- Teach kids basic rules. These could include to share their toys, to control their words when they are angry, and to be gentle when touching animals and people.
- Reward positive habits. Applaud them when toddlers show gentleness and sharing.
- Assist young children to broaden their circle of friends. Pre-schoolers can share their feelings in words and should be urged to make good friends with other kids.
- Organize social events for pre-schoolers. To boost your young child's social communication, host parties in your home. Attend events with other pre-schoolers present, and

welcome your next-door neighbours to drop their young children at your house.

- Teach pre-schoolers to use different words, instead of the words they like. Clarify why this is necessary. Emphasize how it feels for people to be struck, and urge pre-schoolers to apologize if they have actually injured another child's feelings.
- Encourage pre-schoolers to discuss their feelings. Ask them to discuss how they really feel around various other kids and help them to find the words to explain their feelings.

School-Aged Children

Create social skills in school-aged kids. When kids go to school, they have a built-in environment that exposes them to chances to connect with others, to share toys, and to communicate with others about their feelings and needs.

- Display manners. Kids note and imitate grownups. Show them social skills by setting a good example and greeting individuals warmly. Speaking pleasantly to others in times of disagreement will teach children to do the same.
- Expose kids to effective problem-solving methods. When a problem occurs between children, intervene to ask how each child is really feeling. Encourage children to share their feelings with one another, and offer remedies for resolving the problem.
- Teach children to appreciate each other's distinctions and differences. Provide opportunities for youngsters to display their strengths and talents, and encourage an environment in which children praise one another for toughness and positive performance.

Developing social skills in youngsters readies them for a lifetime of healthier interactions in all elements of life.

Useful Ways to Boost Your Child's Social Skills

When most parents think about teaching their child good social skills, they think about seeing to it their child learns to say "please" and "thank you" Others may also teach a youngster to share a snack with their friends during playtime or teach them why it is appropriate to give every child in the class a birthday party invitation and not to leave anybody out. All of these are fantastic social skills for every child to have.

However, for parents of children with an invisible disability—whether it is autism, non-verbal learning disorder, sensory handling problems, or even bipolar disorder—we think about totally different difficulties when we are faced with teaching our children social skills. We consider reciprocal language, sharing control during play, being versatile, and not monopolizing the conversation (that is, assuming they even know how to begin a talk to begin with).

Understanding that our youngsters have these intricate difficulties with social skills makes teaching social skills simply a part of a much bigger problem. Frequently our child's social skills deficits are compounded by other challenges, such as attention issues, sensory concerns, or a basic lack of interest. Yet that does not change the fact that most of our little ones want good friends.

And they really need help from us to make and keep good friends.

So how do you set about helping improve your kid's social capabilities? Good question!

In our home we have actually tried a lot of different ways to demonstrate social skills. These vary from the basic skills (asking someone to enjoy something with you) to the more complex (needing to answer their question before asking another one) to the ones that have no solution whatsoever (the best ways to combat "reasonable"). And for many years, I have actually boiled it down to those that work.

Here are tips for boosting your child's social skills:

Formal Classes. Among the most advantageous things I have done is to show my friend's son online official social skills classes. Ours was taught by a lady with expertise in social work, but many are led by other professionals (speech therapists, educational consultants, and therapists).

At first I thought this was a waste of time and assumed I could do it on my own. I am social, I understand just what to do—but I couldn't have actually been more wrong. The course of study breaks down standard social situations into easy to learn and simple to practice concepts. From ways to behave like a good host and ways to turns while playing, to how to choose and keep good friends, these detailed, simple lessons have actually been invaluable to us.

Social Skills Groups. Once we had several of the basics down, the next step was to exercise them. We go to social skills teams that are "facilitated" but are not "instructed". It is a chance for us to be with other children who have social difficulties and exercise the skills we are discovering. Having me or another facilitator available permits my son to get verbal and nonverbal tips on how to adjust habits, or very simply, when to raise a concern.

Social Stories. Reading stories that demonstrate social circumstances to a child (in pictures or in words depending on their degree of development) provides a child a much better understanding of expected behaviour, recommended speech, and social standards in a particular situation. This is a great way to provide your child some black and white details about this grey topic.

Online Video. Among the most effective means I have found to demonstrate or show these social situations, especially those where my friend's son is on his own (school, birthday parties, play dates) are via online video. There are a lot of videos available, but the ones we have used most frequently are easy to find online. (They even have an iPod/iPad app!)

This is an excellent way to resolve certain problems that are impacting my friend's youngster. "I want to play with my friend's child at their home, but every time I ask him to play tag, he says no." Role playing with our children permits us to come up with other things my friend's child could point out to Johnny without the on-the-sport pressure.

You should organize for your child to take part in this brainstorming session, as his take on the situation will often be astonishingly helpful.

Real Life Technique. There is nothing better than this method. Our kids need to leave home and make mistakes in order to find improvement. Don't stay inside. Do not avoid every party or the community playground. Give it some good thought, and choose a social challenge that will provide your youngster the opportunity to shine—or at least to twinkle a little.

Play Dates. Play dates are the best means to put your child in position to prosper. You control the area, the time, and the play. If his problem is not taking turns, do not play board games.

Phone Conversations. Do not undervalue the need for telephone calls. Probably texting will likely take over from actual phone conversations by the time most of our little ones are young adults, but they really need to understand effective ways to have a discussion on the phone now.

And don't ignore this! It is difficult because there are no visual clues, no way to review gestures. They will have to count on their ability to listen to tone and inflection and respond to questions without a visual cue. It needs practice. Use play phones, call loved ones, or set up telephone calls between play dates with the pals your youngster makes.

Make Up Rules. This is an awkward one, but for those social skills that don't really have any rhyme or reason you have to make up your own. Here's an example:

In situations where he is fighting with his brothers, I have no idea why the "bro code" states that you cannot strike a guy in the back or a few other spots. That is just not appropriate. It is a social standard that I cannot explain. My friend's boy requires direction on these points, and the most effective I can provide him are minimal standards that we can increase as he gets older.

What the principles in this book have given you is not a check for a specific amount but a signed blank check, a check which you may fill out for any amount you wish, i.e., any amount your beliefs can see. These principles have worked time and time again. They are working and they will continue to work. It will be wise to reread the chapter again.

Chapter 14:

CONFIDENCE

Occasionally parents don't relate self-control with teaching confidence, ad many people don't see confidence as a skill. When moms and dads use self-control and not punishment, little ones gain self-esteem and confidence. And learning to be positive means that kids have the ability to learn from blunders, accept criticism, and use positive self-talk to help them find confidence.

When parents develop clear household policies and regular positive and negative outcomes, kids understand just what to expect. When kids really feel protected, they feel more confident about trying new tasks and discovering their abilities. Positive discipline is a terrific way to ensure that children find out how to have self-assurance.

Kids and Self-Esteem

Kids that have a healthy and balanced self-esteem and self-confidence have the tendency to be a lot more resistant in the life's day-to-day battles and to handle all the situations in a positive way. They tend to take care of disputes much better and deal more quickly with the problems they encounter. Healthy and balanced self-esteem is like a shield against all the bad things that happen around children, as opposed to all the difficulties they have to experience.

Children that are self-confident are happier; they appreciate life far more and smile a great deal. They are much more positive and much better anchored. They are realistic and have sane assumptions about life and other people. These children are well adapted to life, and they are able to discover solutions for all the issues.

On the other hand, little ones with reduced self-esteem see in life's challenges a long-term source of anxiety and irritation. Young adults of this type, with a bad self-image, have difficulties in finding solutions for the problems they encounter. They don't respect themselves, and they might have an inferiority complex. If they've got used to thoughts like "I am unable to do this" or "I cannot do anything good," they often become withdrawn and alienate themselves from their peers; they become passive and even dispirited.

When they are dealing with problems or any kind of kind of difficulties, they will usually react with a negative answer. "I can't do that!" "I am not able to do this!" "It's much too much for me."

It is crucial to boost a child and to help him or her rely on his or her abilities, powers, and qualities. A confident youngster will certainly do much more in life, will be well adjusted, and will accomplish many things.

There is a hilarious story about a deaf little frog. All the frogs got together for a contest. The winner was expected to climb a really high tree in the forest. A few frogs started to climb up. The others, who were near the tree, started to say, "They will never ever make it! It's an impossible mission!" One by one all the frogs gave up. Just one little toad remained to climb the tree, and only when it had made it to the top did everyone realize that the little frog was deaf and could not hear all the frustration from the others. It listened to itself and it made it to the top. The moral: Often it's enough to rely on yourself and you will be successful.

It is exactly the same with the self-confidence and self-esteem. In the end, what really matters is the way you think you are. You will certainly make it if you think in a positive way and you trust yourself to do something!

When parents make use of self-control and not punishment, kids gain self-worth and confidence. And learning to be confident means that kids are able to learn from mistakes, accept negative judgments, and use good self-talk to help them find confidence.

When parents set up clear house rules and consistent positive and negative outcomes, kids know exactly what to expect. Good discipline is a fantastic way to make sure that little ones learn just how to have confidence.

On the other hand, children with low self-esteem see in life's obstacles a long-term source of anxiety and disappointment.

What Is Self-Esteem?

Self-esteem is a term used in psychology to describe how we think of our own selves, how we see ourselves. It entails beliefs, feelings, and sensations, and it is a general examination of self. The way we see ourselves influences our motivations, the way we act and react, our mind sets, desires, and, typically, our entire emotional sphere. It's the value we give to our self; it's the self-image we have made about our self.

The pattern of the self-image is developed in early childhood. A little kid that tries for days to make his first steps and fails ultimately succeeds and makes those steps alone. He will really feel encouraged and will develop self-respect. He will gain a positive perspective. "I can!"

In the early stages of development, kids understand that they need to persist and try and try until they succeed. They will attempt and fail, and try once again until they ultimately get what they want. In this way a little one understands just what he can do, just what is he capable of doing, and the amount of work and effort he has to make in order to achieve success.

At the same time, the self-image is also built as a result of one's interaction with others. Healthy relationships will promote a positive self-image and will assist a youngster to develop self-confidence. That's why is essential that parents get involved and provide the support the little one really needs, so the little one will have the ability to develop a proper, healthy, and practical self-image.

Self-respect is built upon our own perception of what we are and the sensation that we are liked and cherished by others. For instance, no matter how good a child may be, if he or she doesn't feel loved and cherished by his parents, he or she will certainly have a low self-esteem and self-confidence.

Similarly, a youngster who knows that he is liked but doesn't have self-confidence may end up having reduced self-esteem. I might say that in order to create healthy and balanced self-esteem, we have to find the equilibrium between passion and success. It's the value we give to ourselves; it's the self-image we have made concerning ourselves.

Healthy and balanced relationships will certainly promote a good self-image and will assist a child to develop self-assurance. That's why it is really crucial that the parents get involved and offer the help the child needs, so the little one will be able to create a proper, sensible, healthy, and balanced self-image.

Identifying Healthy Self-Confidence and Self-Esteem

A well balanced kid with healthy self-esteem:

- Knows that he is making the right choice, even if other don't agree with him (friends, classmates).
- Has his own principles and values and can tell right from wrong.
- Knows that he can solve the problems, do the homework, or participate in different activities.
- Is not worried about the things that he got wrong in the past. He made mistakes but he got over them and now has the courage to try again.
- Feels that he is equal with his peers, friends, and classmates. He doesn't have feelings of inferiority.
- Is sensitive to the feelings and needs of others.

- Knows his qualities and his flaws and accepts them.
- Likes to interact with others.
- Is optimistic.

Identifying Low Self-Confidence and Self-Esteem

A child with low self-esteem:

- Avoids trying new things.
- Is withdrawn.
- Thinks of himself in terms like "I can't do it", "I am stupid", etc.
- Is not tolerant about situations that are frustrating.
- Gives up quickly when things are not going the way he wants.
- Is very critical of himself, but at the same time is very sensitive about the criticism of others.
- Is always worrying and has a constant fear that he will make a mistake or he will make a fool of himself.
- Is defensive and irritable.
- Is envious of others and invidious.
- Is pessimistic.

How to Help Your Child Have Self-Esteem and Be Self-Confident

- When he is doing good things, compliment your child and praise him. This way he will gain self-confidence. When you are upset or dissatisfied with him, be very careful how you speak with him and exactly what words you choose to use. Words can hurt a little one's self-confidence and self-esteem more than anything else.

Always be a good role model! Little ones discover by imitation, so they will act like you do, and they will certainly react the same way they have seen you react.

- Identify and deal with incorrect opinions your youngster is having about himself. Teach him to be realistic and not to be too tough on himself when he makes errors. No one is perfect!

- Use your affection to support your kid and make him see how important and cherished he is. By doing this he will build self-esteem much faster.
- Offer him realistic feedback. When he is wrong or has done something bad, do not hurt his feelings and criticize him in a basic way. It's very wrong to use sentences like "You are not capable of anything!"
- Don't be judgmental.
- See to it that he is really feeling safe and loved in your home. Little ones who have been abused or molested have extremely reduced self-esteem and no self-assurance.
- Teach your child that a healthy self-confidence is not the same as being egotistical with the others.
- Motivate your kids to make their own decisions. You can guide them, but they need to decide on their own.
- Do not establish unrealistic expectations for your children.
- When he fails in something, Make sure your youngster is still feeling approved.

Talk to Your Child Early Enough

Talking about menstruation or wet dreams after they have actually started means you're late. Answer the earliest concerns kids have about their bodies, such as the differences between boys and girls and where babies come from. Do not overload them with details; simply answer their questions. If you have no idea of the answer, help them locate a person who does, like a trusted friend.

You understand your kids. You can hear when your youngster's beginning to tell jokes about sex or when her attention to her personal looks is increasing. This is an opportune time to jump in with your own concerns.

- Are you noticing any changes in your body?
- Are you having any strange feelings?
- Are you sad sometimes and don't know why?

An examination can serve as a jumping-off point for a great parent/child discussion. The later you wait to have this discussion, the more likely your child will be to form mistaken beliefs or become embarrassed about or terrified of bodily and psychological changes.

In addition, the earlier you open free lines of interaction, the better chance you have of keeping them open during the teen years. Offer your kid publications about puberty created for children who are entering it. Share memories of your own adolescence. There's nothing like understanding that a parent went through it too to make a youngster feel more secure.

Inform Your Teen and Stay Informed Yourself

The teen years usually are a time of testing, and often that testing consists of high-risk behaviours. Don't avoid the topics of sex, alcoholic beverages, drugs, and tobacco use. Discussing these things freely with children before they're exposed to them boosts the chance that they'll act responsibly when the moment comes. Share your family values with your teen and discuss just what you believe is right and wrong.

Know your child's friends and understand their friends' parents. Regular communication between moms and dads can go a long way toward developing a safe atmosphere for all adolescents in a peer group. Moms and dads could help each other monitor the kids' activities without making the little ones feel that they're being watched.

Put Yourself in Your Child's Place

Practice empathy by helping your child understand that it's normal to be a bit concerned or self-conscious, and that it's okay to feel grown up one minute and like a kid the next.

Choose Your Fights

It may appear crazy, but to the most of your potential, enable your teen to have even more freedom. Does she want to put eco-friendly red stripes in her hair? As long as school is okay with it, give her that flexibility. Eco-friendly hair will certainly discolour, and some day it will grow out. Your adolescent's attempts at becoming a person are essential. Figuring out who they are—that's the work of a teen. Also, when you can allow your adolescent some independence to make choices and endure the consequences of their choices, it teaches them most lasting lessons. Life becomes your adolescent's finest teacher.

If teenagers intend to colour their hair, paint their fingernails black, or wear funky clothing, think again before you object. Teenagers want to shock their moms and dads, and it's a whole lot better to let them do something short-term and benign. Leave the objections for things that really matter, like tobacco, drugs and alcohol, or long-term changes to their appearance.

Ask why your teen wants to dress up or try to look different in order to understand how your teenager is really feeling. If they look different, help your teen understand how he or she may be viewed. You might also wish to discuss how others may perceive them.

Know the Warning Signs

If you think that your adolescent is using drugs or drinking alcoholic beverages, having sex, or really feeling suicidal or depressed, you must step in and take control. It is one thing for your boy to repaint the walls of his room black. It's another when he appears down and talks about suicide. Black walls could indicate he enjoys "emo" music. Discussing self-destruction needs to be taken seriously as a sign of things come. He might get angry and say he hates you for having him reviewed by a mental health and wellness expert, but you may simply be saving his life. If you think your adolescent is damaging himself or herself in ways that are long-term or significant, call your primary healthcare service provider or the neighbourhood crisis hotline number. If you believe your adolescent is in danger, you should be the authority.

A certain amount of adjustment might be typical during the teen years, but a major or lasting change in personality or habits may indicate genuine trouble—the kind that really needs expert help. Watch for these indications:

- Extreme weight gain or loss
- Sleep problems
- Rapid, drastic changes in personality
- Sudden change in friends
- Skipping school continually
- Falling grades
- Talk or even jokes about suicide
- Signs of tobacco, alcohol, or drug use
- Run-ins with the law

Other inappropriate behaviour that lasts for more than six weeks can be a sign of an underlying problem. You can expect a glitch or two in your teen's behaviour and grades during this time, but your A/B pupil should not all of a sudden be failing, and your generally extrovert children shouldn't all of a sudden become continuously withdrawn. Your medical professional or a neighbourhood therapist, psychologist, or psychiatrist can help you find proper guidance.

Respect Kids' Privacy

Some moms and dads, naturally, have a very hard time with this one. They may really feel that anything their kids do is their business. To help your teen become a young grownup, you'll need to grant some personal privacy. You should enter your child's privacy until you get to the heart of the trouble if you see warning signs of problems. Otherwise, it's an excellent suggestion to back off.

In other words, your young adult's room, texts, e-mails, and phone calls need to be private. You also should not expect your teenager to share all thoughts or tasks with you at all times. Certainly, for safety reasons, you need to constantly understand where adolescents are going, when they'll be returning, exactly what they're doing, and whom they are with, but you do not need to know every detail. And you certainly should not expect to be invited along!

Begin with trust. Let your teen know that you trust him or her. If the trust gets broken, he or she may enjoy less freedom until trust is rebuilt.

Monitor What Kids See and Read

Television, books, shows, and publications, the Net—little ones have access to lots of info. Recognize just what your little ones watch and read. Do not be afraid to establish restrictions on the amount of time spent facing the computer or the TV. Know exactly what they're learning from the media and what they could be communicating with online.

Teenagers should not have unlimited access to TV or the Net in private. These need to be public tasks. Access to technology needs also to be limited after specific hours (say, after 10 PM or so) to encourage ample sleep. It's not unreasonable to have wireless phone and computer systems off limits at times.

Get Your Child a Role Model

Always keep in mind that children learn from what you do, so be a positive role model. Your actions are important

Parents are a young adult's main example, regardless of the powerful impacts of peers and the media. The way you respond to your youngster's worries about body image can sway their mind set and behaviours. Tips include:

- Set a good example. Do not crash diet or skip meals. Educate your child about the risks of unhealthy eating practices.
- Do not react negatively to their choices. Young adults like to experiment with meal choices. For example, some young adults may want to try being vegetarian. Try to appreciate your child's choice and help them to prepare a vegetarian diet regimen that includes all the important nutrients.
- Improve your youngster's self-worth. Motivate them in exercises that help them to cherish exactly what their body can do, instead of just what it looks like. Studies show that higher self-confidence can shield a teenager against damaging behaviours such as crash dieting.
- Educate your youngster about the convincing marketing approaches of commercials and advertisements.
- Motivate your kid to learn about health problems and take responsibility for their own mind set and habits. A persistent young adult may dismiss your suggestions about nourishment. Nevertheless, they might respond with more enthusiasm if you offer them access to information from reliable and independent resources such as your medical professional or the Better Health Channel.
- If they are attempting to lose weight, do not assume that your child is eating a lot less. The end of a development surge often triggers a drop in cravings.
- The way you react to your kid's physical body picture concerns can sway their habits and perspectives.
- Enhance your child's confidence.
- Encourage your youngster to find out about health issues and take charge of their very own perspectives and habits.

Be a Good Role Model

The most important example in your kid's life is you. Parents can encourage their children to really feel good about themselves by showing them just how it's done. For example:

- Children learn eating behaviours from their moms and dads, so make certain you include lots of fresh fruits, vegetables, lean meats, low-fat dairy items, and unprocessed cereals in the family's diet. Go easy on takeaway, fried foods, and sweet treats.
- Do not crash diet. Do not motivate your child to crash diet either. Research reveals that many young people believe that crash dieting is an effective and harmless way to reduce weight. Get in touch with your child about the risks of crash diets. Visit the Better Health Network to find out more on this.
- Approve your own physical body's shape and form. Don't complain about "unsightly" body components, or at least do not share your opinions with your child.
- Accept other people's physical body sizes and shapes. Don't pay a lot of attention to physical looks, or your kid will do so as well. Rather, try to speak to your child about all the different aspects that make up a person, such as character, abilities, and attitude to life.
- Work out frequently. Have at least one family activity per week that includes some kind of exercise—for instance, walking, dance, playing yard cricket, taking a stroll, or swimming.
- Be wary of media communications and photos that promote slimness. Encourage your youngster to question and block out Western society's slender "beauty ideal".

Things to Remember

There are some kids who are really prepared to take care of everything in their lives. In these little ones, the front part of their brain is established early, permitting them to be highly functional people. Not all kids are like this, and if you are comparing your youngster to these kids, therein could lie the issue. A lot of children do not grow this part of their brain until after adolescence. If you hang in there, you just could find that they improve on their own, in time and with maturity.

Obviously, you should always make certain that your youngster does not have a learning disability or any other illness that could be keeping him from succeeding academically. Start by having a discussion with your youngster's paediatrician and go from there. As soon as you have actually taken care of that issue, simply recognize that no two kids are the same. Every person discovers things in different ways, and you may need to work really hard to discover just what type your youngster is. Sticking carefully to the actions mentioned above will help get you and your kid on a much less troubled path to success.

The trick to helping your child past this lies in all of the other steps above—positive reinforcement, encouragement, and framework. Not all kids are like this, and if you are contrasting your youngster to one of these children, therein might lie in the trouble.

KEY POINTS

- Remember to communicate with your child.
- Review your expectations and then take action.
- Respect your kid's privacy.
- Recognize his or her strength and weaknesses.
- Be a good role model for your child.
- Appreciate your child for who he is, not for who you pictured he would be.
- Be clear in describing expectations.
- Remember to be involved with your child. Your opinion and support still matter.
- Make time during the day or evening to listen to your teen's activities. Be sure that she understands you are definitely interested and listening closely to what she says.
- Discuss ways to manage and handle tension.
- Listen more than you talk. Bear in mind that we are each given two ears and one mouth.
- Avoid sarcasm, criticism, and yelling.
- Know where your teen is and whether a responsible adult is present. Make an agreement with her about when she will call you, where you can find her, and exactly what time you expect her home.
- Do not compare your kid with any other kids. Every child is unique.

You can really make every day of this life a joyous experience. Reread the book again. It will open new perspectives in your life.

Use the techniques presented in this book and tell others about the good things you learned and experienced from this book.

All right! You are being given the green light. Get set! Go!

ABOUT THE AUTHOR

Mr Anish was born on an Island called Diu. His childhood was mostly spent with his grandparents, as his parents were in Portugal. Every evening his grandpa used to meet his four or five friends near the seashore and talk about life and their experiences. Anish used to play in the sand, making castles and listening to their conversations.

Anish had to teach his younger sister during school. He was constantly reading many books. He'd go to the library and spend countless hours just reading books on any subject.

Later He went to Portugal and was living with the parents for five years. He learned Portuguese over there. His passion for reading books and going to libraries was still alive. In his free time he was mostly in the library reading or on the Internet finding articles to read. Later he decided he want to go to the United Kingdom, and managed to get there with friends' help. On the start he was babysitting his cousin kids and later his friends. He learned a lot and decided to share with everyone.

About the Book

Raising a baby, especially for the first time, is both interesting and tough. This is a time for developing the bonds that will last a lifetime, giving the child the internal resources to create self-esteem and the ability to connect positively with others.

How to Greatly Influence Your Child While Parenting will assist you in solving problems with your child. You will be making the right decisions for your child in creating ways and means of great achievement. With the techniques in this book, you can sleep on it and awake in the morning with answers so clear-cut you will be amazed!

It is likewise time for parents to start to discover who this new individual really is. Each child is unique, and it is vital that moms and dads learn to know, regard, support, and encourage the distinct qualities and potentials of each youngster.

My main reason for writing this book is to help parents understand what their child needs and wants and what to expect as the child grows from a baby to adolescent.

Some information you will gain from this book is as follows:

- Tips for parenting during the teen years
- Understanding the stages from birth to adolescence
- Communicating with young children
- Tips to get your kid talking
- What to do to change a child's behaviour
- Tips on teaching your teen how to deal with stress
- Helping children deal with their anger
- Tips on teaching kids about money

Thank you and I suggest to reread the book as it will help to understand it better and give better perspective.